P9-CFY-444

MEDICAL LIBRARY
NORTH MEMORIAL HEALTH CARE
3300 OAKDALE AVENUE NORTH
ROBBINSDALE, MN 55422-2900

MEDICAL LIBRARY
NORTH MEMORIAL HEALTH CARE
3300 OAKDALE AVENUE NORTH
ROBBINSDALE, MN 55422-2900

Designing the Customer-Centric Organization

MEDICAL LIBRARY
NORTH MEMORIAL HEALTH CARE
3300 OAKDALE AVENUE NORTH
ROBBINSDALE, MN 55422-2900

Jay R. Galbraith

Designing the Customer-Centric Organization

A Guide to Strategy, Structure, and Process

MEDICAL LIBRARY
NORTH MEMORIAL HEALTH CARE
3300 OAKDALE AVENUE NORTH
ROBBINSDALE, MN 55422-2900

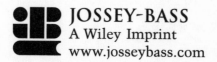

JOSSEY-BASS
A Wiley Imprint
www.josseybass.com

HF5415
G148d

Copyright © 2005 by Jay R. Galbraith.

Published by Jossey-Bass
A Wiley Imprint
989 Market Street, San Francisco, CA 94103-1741   www.josseybass.com

No part of this publication may be reproduced, stored in a retrieval system, or transmitted in any form or by any means, electronic, mechanical, photocopying, recording, scanning, or otherwise, except as permitted under Section 107 or 108 of the 1976 United States Copyright Act, without either the prior written permission of the Publisher, or authorization through payment of the appropriate per-copy fee to the Copyright Clearance Center, Inc., 222 Rosewood Drive, Danvers, MA 01923, 978-750-8400, fax 978-750-4470, or on the web at www.copyright.com. Requests to the Publisher for permission should be addressed to the Permissions Department, John Wiley & Sons, Inc., 111 River Street, Hoboken, NJ 07030, 201-748-6011, fax 201-748-6008, e-mail: permcoordinator@wiley.com.

Jossey-Bass books and products are available through most bookstores. To contact Jossey-Bass directly call our Customer Care Department within the U.S. at 800-956-7739, outside the U.S. at 317-572-3986, or fax 317-572-4002.

Jossey-Bass also publishes its books in a variety of electronic formats. Some content that appears in print may not be available in electronic books.

Library of Congress Cataloging-in-Publication Data

Galbraith, Jay R.
   Designing the customer-centric organization : a guide to strategy, structure, and process / Jay R. Galbraith.
       p. cm.—(The Jossey-Bass business & management series)
   Includes bibliographical references and index.
   ISBN 0-7879-7919-8 (alk. paper)
   1. Customer relations—Management—Handbooks, manuals, etc.   2. Strategic planning—Handbooks, manuals, etc.   I. Title.   II. Series.
   HF5415.5.G345 2005
   658.8'12—dc22

                                                                   2005001675

Printed in the United States of America
FIRST EDITION
HB Printing   10 9 8 7 6 5 4 3 2 1

15888

The Jossey-Bass
Business & Management Series

Contents

Preface

This book is the result of several testy arguments that arose with some long-term clients. When similarly contentious arguments began cropping up in executive development programs, I had to reflect on what was happening. In every case, I was diagnosing a company to be product-centric and not customer-centric—which I was suggesting that it become. The clients took offense because, in their minds, they were customer-centric: they had been working for years to understand and please their customers. I was accusing them of being product-centric, and they respectfully objected. When I persisted, they testily objected. The content of this book is the result of my attempts to help these clients become truly customer-centric— particularly when they think they already are.

A historical perspective gave me a better understanding of my clients' objections. Companies in the 1960s and '70s—espousing clichés like "The customer is always right"—also believed that they paid attention to the customer. This perception was first shattered by customer preference for higher-quality Japanese products and then by the appearance of *In Search of Excellence* (1981), whose authors, Peters and Waterman, showed that excellent companies were "close to the customer" and articulated in detail how excellent companies got that way, with practices that far exceeded those of most companies.

Companies now began in earnest to put the customer at the top of their priority list. They defined quality as the customer defined it. They used focus groups to better understand customer preferences. They designed products to be more customer-friendly. They tracked their progress by continually measuring customer satisfaction. A language developed around becoming "close to the customer" and "customer-focused." By the end of the 1980s and early '90s, many companies believed that they were market-oriented, customer-focused, or customer-driven. This is the belief that I encountered in my sea of contentious confrontations. The clients felt that they had been working for over a decade on putting the customer center stage. "How could we not be customer-centric?" they asked. Well, let us count the ways . . .

The capabilities required for true customer-centricity go far beyond just placing the customer prominently on the company radar screen. They incorporate the work that most companies have undertaken for the past ten to fifteen years to become customer-focused, and build on them in specific and sometimes foundation-shaking means. This book represents the hard work, the challenges, and the ultimate successes involved in bringing my product-centric clients into their optimal levels of customer-centricity.

While these discussions with my clients were taking place, I ran across Nathaniel Foote, who was leading McKinsey's organization design practice. He was working with Russ Eisenstat from the Center for Organizational Fitness. They were interested in the customer dimension of organization, but from the point of view of adding another dimension to an already complex structure. Their project was called "Managing Multiple Dimensions." Many of McKinsey's clients were experiencing the moves to customer-centricity, and the consulting teams were asking for help. I joined them, along with Danny Miller, Quentin Hope, and Charles Heckscher, in a research effort to understand the challenges of managing customers, product lines, geographies, and functions under one corporate umbrella.

My part of the effort was to conduct data collection in the form of case studies. I conducted fourteen studies of companies that were enhancing the customer dimension of their organizations. (In the language of this book, they were creating a customer-centric capability and adding it to their existing structures.) This book is a direct response to conducting these case studies, and the clarifications that came from follow-up discussions with the research team. My thanks to Nathaniel Foote, now with the Center for Organizational Fitness, and McKinsey for their support during that period.

Breckenridge, Colorado   Jay R. Galbraith
February 2005

The Author

Jay Galbraith, an internationally recognized expert on organization design, helps major global corporations create capability for competing. His work focuses on organizational design, change, and development; strategy and organization at the corporate, business unit, and international levels; and international partnering arrangements, including joint ventures and network-type organizations. He is currently examining organizational units that are rapidly reconfigurable to suit quickly changing demands of customers and markets across multinational boundaries. Galbraith consults regularly with international clients in the United States, Europe, Asia, South Africa, and South America.

Galbraith is a senior research scientist at the Center for Effective Organizations at the University of Southern California (USC) and professor emeritus at the International Institute for Management Development in Lausanne, Switzerland. Prior to joining the faculty at USC, he directed his own management consulting firm. He has previously been on the faculty of the Wharton School at the University of Pennsylvania and the Sloan School of Management at MIT.

Galbraith has written numerous articles for professional journals, handbooks, and research collections. His recently revised book, *Designing Organizations: An Executive Guide to Strategy, Structure and Process* (Jossey-Bass, 2002), is a balanced perspective of organization design principles, structures, and processes written for the executive manager. Galbraith, along with Diane Downey and Amy Kates, has produced a very practical workbook for organization designers, *Designing Dynamic Organizations* (Amacom, 2002). His book *Designing the Global Corporation* (Jossey-Bass, 2000) describes how leading multinational corporations address the demands of their increasingly global customers to provide solutions, not just products. *Tomorrow's Organization: Crafting Winning Capabilities in a Dynamic World* (Jossey-Bass, 1998), was a cooperative project with Sue Mohrman, Edward E. Lawler III, and the Center for Effective Organizations. It is a solution-oriented guidebook for creating organizations capable of competing in the next century. *Competing with Flexible Lateral Organizations* (Addison-Wesley, 1994) explores management through less hierarchical team structures. Galbraith's award-winning *Organizing for the Future* (Jossey-Bass, 1993) is a compilation of ten years of research done by the Center for Effective Organizations. Prior publications include *Strategy Implementation: The Role of Structure and Process* (with Rob Kazanjian, West Publishing, 1986); "Designing the Innovative Organization" in *Organization Dynamics* (Winter 1982); "Human Resources and Organization Planning" in *Human Resource Management*; *Designing Complex Organizations* (Addison-Wesley, 1973); and *Organization Design* (Addison-Wesley, 1977). Galbraith's recent working papers include "Managing the New Complexity," "The Front-Back Organization: A New Organizational Hybrid," "Designing a Reconfigurable Organization," and "Organizing Around the Customer."

Designing the Customer-Centric Organization

INTRODUCTION

In order to be a successful and viable firm in the twenty-first century, a company must have a customer-centric capability. The early movers will gain a competitive advantage, while stragglers will scramble for a competitive necessity.

In most industries today, it is difficult to make money by just selling products and services to customers. Stand-alone products and services commoditize rapidly and collapse profit margins. The new foundation of profitability is the customer relationship. Indeed, some suggest that Wall Street will be evaluating companies based on the total value of their customer relationships (Seybold, 2001; Selden and Colvin, 2003). This thinking results from studies that show that sales to existing customers are more profitable than sales to new customers. It costs more to acquire new customers, and they are more likely to switch. Most desirable is a loyal, long-term customer who has a relationship with the company. But to be effective, customer loyalty and relationships have to be managed; companies need to organize around these loyal customers.

Today, nobody owns the customer. The customer owns you. The customer may want to talk to the salesperson or to the distributor. The customer may want to talk directly to the service department. He or she may want to deal face-to-face or by telephone, fax, or e-mail. And a customer who poses a question or complaint by e-mail expects the salesperson to provide an answer to the query during their next face-to-face meeting. If the salesperson cannot answer the question, the customer sees no relationship. To have a relationship, the company needs to be able to do business the way the customer wishes.

Different customers want to do business differently, and being profitable today means having the capabilities that allow for malleability. It means forming long-term relationships with the most valuable customers. It means interacting with these customers across multiple points of contact and integrating the results of these contacts into a consistent company position for the customer. It means learning from the contacts to customize the company's offerings for different customer segments. It means learning about new customer needs and expanding the company's offering to meet them. It means using knowledge of customers to package products and services into solutions that create value for the customers.

And doesn't *that* sound like a lot of work! Many firms are reluctant or unwilling to make the organizational changes necessary to build a customer-centric capability; the preference thus far has been to keep it simple and create simple, autonomous business units that control their resources and can be accountable for their performance. In other words: keep it simple for *management*.

But that kind of simplicity means making it difficult for the customer. It is then up to the customer or some third party to do the integrating and capture the value of serving the customer. Keeping it simple for management leaves money on the table for more complex organizations to capture. By implementing a customer-centric capability, the company can now keep it simple for the customer, eliminating third-party solutions and redirecting that errant cash flow.

Why would firms hesitate to create a more profitable organization by building customer-centricity? Beyond fiscal myopia, which motivates companies to ignore implementation altogether, it appears to be a combination of two factors. One is an underestimation of the changes needed to implement customer-centric systems, such as customer relationship management (CRM) software. Management cannot simply insert a CRM system into a product-centric organization and expect to capitalize on customer relationships. Early returns show that half of all CRM implementations fail to achieve the expected results, and one in five actually damages customer relationships (Kehoe, 2002). Once again, we have to relearn the fact that organizations are complex human systems into which new technology must be painstakingly introduced.

The second factor that limits the time and energy invested by management is the belief that they are already customer-centric. For the past ten or fifteen years, these firms have been working hard to become "close to the customer" or "customer focused." While acknowledging that this work has been necessary and useful, it does not make the company customer-centric. To be customer-centric, a firm must literally organize around the customer.

The purpose of this book is to articulate what it means to be customer-centric and to illustrate how to organize accordingly. Chapter One addresses the inherent differences between customer-centric and product-centric capabilities. It also explores the reasons the customer dimension has come to such prominence and examines the structures and philosophies involved in implementing a customer-centric application, as well as addressing the frequent aversion to implementation.

Chapter Two details the different types of customer relationship strategies and provides a strategy locator to determine the level of customer-centricity—if any—that would best serve your company. The capability can be broken down into low, medium, and high levels of implementation, with tools offered to ascertain the appropriate level. Finally, lateral relationships, with an overview of informal groups versus the more complex forms of management, are discussed.

Now that the groundwork has been established, Chapter Three begins the process of implementation. The specific elements required for applying the lightest version of the capability are introduced, making sure the reader understands that all of these elements, plus others, will be necessary for companies that require medium- or high-level applications. In addition, two case studies are provided of companies that required this level of implementation.

Chapter Four details the next, more-intensive level and the elements that must be added for its implementation. A case study of a target medium-level corporation is provided.

Chapter Five gives an in-depth look at IBM, considered by many (including me) to be the best success story of customer-centric application. Both the tribulations and the triumphs of this flourishing giant are examined to provide readers with illumination and inspiration as they trudge the sometimes rocky road of corporate reinvention.

Chapter Six gives three more successful examples of companies that have made a successful transition along with their change processes.

Chapter Seven is a case study of a semiconductor company that moves from a completely product-centric organization to an organization with a customer-centric solutions unit. It provides a good discussion of the process for designing a solutions organization.

Chapter Eight completes the book with a description of the management processes through which strong leadership is exercised.

1

SURVIVING THE CUSTOMER REVOLUTION

In this chapter you will learn:

- That being customer-centric means literally organizing around the customer.

- The complete definition of organization (it's more than just structure).

- The definition of a customer-centric organization and its contrast to a product-centric organization.

- How your organization compares to a complete customer-centric design.

- How customer-centric your organization really is.

For better or worse, one fact has become increasingly clear over the past ten years: the marketplace is customer driven. The days of customers chanting, "We'll take what you offer," have been replaced with an expectant, "Give us what we'd like, with a side order of customization."

The power in the buyer-seller interaction has been moving systematically to the buyer. In many industries, global competition and industry overcapacity have given buyers more choice, and they are learning how to use it. Electronic commerce and information transparency have reduced seller knowledge advantages. Authors such as Patricia Seybold even see the Internet as starting a "customer revolution" (Seybold, 2001), with "customers . . . wresting control away from suppliers and dictating the new business practices for the digital age" (p. xv). The competitive game has clearly shifted to one of pleasing an increasingly more global, knowledgeable, and powerful customer.

The need for customer-centricity is not going away, and it is up to each company to determine the level of application—and hierarchical restructuring—required for success in this morphing marketplace.

The Status Quo Has to Go

The product-centric mind-set is an entrenched one and, like the pit bull, does not relinquish dominance easily. Because it has been the application of choice for so long, managers may even be fooled into believing they are leaving it behind in favor of customer-centric applications, when in fact product-centricity continues running the show with merely a cosmetic gloss of customer focus sprinkled around the edges.

The ideas presented in this book are challenging, particularly in the amount of reorganization they demand from the status quo product-centric corporation. While acknowledging the need for a new customer-centric capability, many companies, tensely watching their financial bottom line, may be tempted to apply a "fingertip" version of the capability to their current structure. It may seem to be the most prudent course of action to dabble in a cursory commitment or apply a cosmetic overlay that seems to do the job.

It cannot be stressed enough how detrimental this toe-in-the-water mind-set can be. A company that truly requires a customer-centric capability will not achieve its goals without its full integration. It is not fiscally prudent at all to go halfway, since it will almost certainly be funds wasted in their entirety. In fact, this approach may end up costing the company more than just its initial wasted investment; the harm done to the workings of the entire structure by an incomplete capability at this level of importance can be enormous, leaving a company bereft in areas well beyond its original need for customer-centricity. It will undoubtedly leave disappointed customers behind whose trust will be difficult to earn back.

The Bottom Line

The bottom line about your bottom line is that customer centricity pays off. For some time, academic studies and consultant studies have demonstrated that being market driven or customer loyalty focused results in higher profitability. The most complete discussion of customer-centered profitability is by Selden and Colvin (2003), who argue that superior results come from managing your business as a portfolio of customers. That means computing the profitability of customers, segmenting them on a profitability basis, and then organizing around those segments. They present a good process for getting started on a customer-centric strategy and the attendant financial systems. This book presents a complete guide to organization design to implement this path to superior economic performance.

Let's Get Fiscal

Let us examine the financial ramifications. By satisfying a customer who wants to use relationships, the customer-centric firm becomes more profitable. Academic research, using the term *market driven* rather than *customer-centric*, shows strong relationships between being market-driven and profitability, sales growth, and new-product success (Narver and Slater, 1998).

Also, the company that implements a customer-centric capability is situated to steer commissions away from the previously required third-party process suppliers, not to mention winning business over other companies that have themselves already become competitively customer-centric.

The final coup may be the largest. Studies argue that the most profitable customer is the existing loyal customer (Reicheld, 1996; Seybold, 1998). Indeed, Seybold (2001) predicts that in the customer economy, investors will value companies based on the sum of the values of their customer relationships. Customer loyalty becomes incrementally more certain as customer-centricity is implemented. With the tight, customized relationships—the "virtuous circle"—established using applied customer solutions, repeat business becomes more and more dependable in an otherwise harshly competitive and fickle marketplace.

Mind over Mind-Set

When you have determined in Chapter Two the level of customer-centricity that your company requires, it is in your best interest to commit to that level and no less. Regardless of the level of application your firm requires, your managerial mind-sets require a high-level commitment; even if the implementation proceeds at the recommended level, it can be sabotaged in ways both subtle and blatant by a crew that has not gotten onboard.

Mind-set is important to successful customer-centrization. The manager whose thought processes are mired in the past is destined to venture forth halfheartedly, if at all. Not only is a clear and positive outlook essential to committing to the proper degree of application, a robust and eager anticipation is needed as implementation unfolds. This may sound like a recommendation to chant positive affirmations to compensate for a gloomy outlook. On the contrary, it is an invitation to discover exactly how promising this process is and how little downside is involved. Once the win-win nature of the capability becomes clear, a robust positivity should enter the psyche without effort.

The Customer-Centric Imperative

In this increasingly customer-driven environment, the call for a customer-centric capability rings out loud and clear. As the expectations and requirements of the customer become more pronounced and complex, the casual customer-focused behaviors of the past grind toward a forced obsolescence. What was once an option is now an imperative.

Consequently, there has been an increase in the strategic priority assigned to the customer dimension of the business, with many companies now organizing around the customer. Creating customer-facing organizational units is a challenge because these companies have structures that are still based predominantly on business units, countries, and functions. It is essential that companies not be tied to their past structures, to the detriment of their existing needs.

Product-Centric versus Customer-Centric

The best way to understand where we need to go is to get a clear picture of where we've been. The contrast between the product- and customer-centric organizations is shown in Table 1.1.

As the table shows, a product-centric company tries to find as many uses and customers as possible for its product. In contrast, a customer-centric company tries to find as many products as possible for its customer, and it has to integrate those products.

From this basic strategic difference, other different organizational features flow. Product-centric companies are structured around product profit centers called business units. Information is collected around products. Business reviews focus discussions around product lines. The customer-centric company is structured around customer segments. Information is collected and profits measured around customer categories. Management discussions are focused on customers. There are similar contrasts around processes, performance measures, human resource policies, and management mind-sets.

Perhaps the most striking difference is that a customer-centric unit is on the side of the customer in a transaction. A server salesperson at IBM is on the side of the seller—the product-centric server business. However, the outsourcing and consulting people at IBM will suggest a Hewlett-Packard server if it makes more sense for the customer. In order to maintain credibility with the customer, the people from the customer-centric global services business must not be biased toward IBM equipment. They must be on the side of the customer in the buyer-seller transaction. More than any other feature, this bias creates a permanent tension between product and customer units.

The argument above has painted the extremes of product- and customer-centricity. Not every solution provider will require the extreme end of this organizational capability; the application can take

Table 1.1 Product-Centric versus Customer-Centric

		Product-Centric Company	Customer-Centric Company
Strategy	Goal	Best product for customer	Best solution for customer
	Main offering	New products	Personalized packages of products, service, support, education, consulting
	Value creation route	Cutting-edge products, useful features, new applications	Customizing for best total solution
	Most important customer	Most advanced customer	Most profitable, loyal customer
	Priority-setting basis	Portfolio of products	Portfolio of customers—customer profitability
	Pricing	Price to market	Price for value, risk
Structure	Organizational concept	Product profit centers, product reviews, product teams	Customer segments, customer teams, customer P&Ls
Processes	Most important process	New product development	Customer relationship management and solutions development
Rewards	Measures	• Number of new products • Percentage of revenue from products less than two years old • Market share	• Customer share of most valuable customer • Customer satisfaction • Lifetime value of a customer • Customer retention
People	Approach to personnel	Power to people who develop products • Highest reward is working on next most challenging product • Manage creative people through challenges with a deadline	Power to people with in-depth knowledge of customer's business • Highest rewards to relationship managers who save the customer's business
	Mental process	Divergent thinking: *How many possible uses of this product?*	Convergent thinking: *What combination of products is best for this customer?*
	Sales bias	On the side of the seller in a transaction	On the side of the buyer in a transaction
	Culture	New product culture: open to new ideas, experimentation	Relationship management culture: searching for more customer needs to satisfy

Source: This table is a composite of points describing product- and customer-centric companies taken from Peppers and Rogers (1993, 1997, 2001), Treacy and Wiersema (1995), Seybold (1998, 2001).

many forms. It should be noted that the more complex a form is necessary, the greater is the accompanying lateral networking capability will be required to expedite functionality. Chapter Two delineates and helps readers define the level of customer-centric application they require; the requisite lateral networking capability is examined in Chapter Two as well.

The balance of this chapter further delineates the customer-centric capability, pinpointing customer needs and desires and the methods to address them. It then provides a model for strategy and organization.

The Rise of the Customer Dimension

Motivated by the increasing buyer-power influence—and the correct thinking that this is where longevity, competitive edge, and financial profitability lie—most industries are addressing the increasing strategic importance of the customer. The specific factors causing this increase vary with the industry, but either individually or collectively, all businesses are experiencing these factors:

- The globalization of the customer
- The preference of customers for partnerships or relationships
- The rise of e-commerce
- The customer's desire for solutions

Globalization

Since 1985, the process of globalization has been driven by increasing amounts of foreign direct investment. The result is that more companies, and therefore more customers, have a direct presence in more countries. Often these global customers—preferred customers in existing countries—object to receiving marginal treatment from a supplier's subsidiary on entering a new country. These customers want a consistent and consistently high level of service in all countries where they are serviced. Indeed, one supplier was chastised by a customer who had been dealing with thirty-seven sales forces providing thirty-seven different standards of service.

The global customer is creating pressure on suppliers to coordinate across countries and businesses. This desire for cross-unit coordination can also be an advantage for the supplier. For example, ABB was an early mover into many countries, Eastern Europe in particular, and now uses its extensive presence to host and provide services to its customers as they enter new countries in which ABB is already present.

Customer Relationships

The pressure for coordination across existing structures is even greater when customers want partnerships or relationships with their suppliers. Professional services firms are finding that clients want one or two global advertising agencies, auditors, cash management banking suppliers, and outsourcers for information technology. In most industries, customers are preferring fewer suppliers in order to establish closer, longer-term relationships. For suppliers, these global partnerships mean a coordination of all countries in which the customer desires integrated services.

Electronic Commerce

E-commerce is another integrating force that can be used to focus on the customer. When a company with a single brand uses its Web site as its storefront, it presents a single face to the customer. The Web site should be designed around the customer's needs, not around the supplier's product capabilities. The site should be designed to do business the way the customer wants to do business. In order to appear as a single company to the customer, the company needs to integrate its businesses, subsidiaries, channels, and functions.

Another integrating force is the management of interactivity with customers. Electronic connectivity with customers allows the company to recognize and remember each customer, interact with them and remember more about them, and then customize the company's offerings based on the knowledge of the customer. Most companies, however, have not mastered integrated customer interactions. Interactivity requires the management of dialogues and content across all media with which the company interacts with the customer: Web site, e-mail, call center, salespersons, service representatives, and so on. The dialogue needs to be managed over time. The last contact with the customer needs to be remembered, along with the last issue of concern and how it was resolved. The resolution needs to be recorded, and the next dialogue must commence from there. All contacts and issues are to be remembered. The idea of interactivity is to collect and integrate all data across all functions, subsidiaries, and product lines in order to get a complete picture of each customer's value and needs. Only then can the company react as a single company and be seen by the customer as a single company. The customer then receives a consistent brand experience across all the touch points with the company.

Solutions

Perhaps the driving factor now facing suppliers is the growing customer preference for solutions or systems instead of stand-alone products. To be sure, customers still order truckloads of desktops from computer manufacturers, but they are also ordering trading rooms or call centers. At IBM, these solutions require the integration of multiple business units in multiple countries with multiple outside suppliers. These solutions are not simply multiple stand-alone products that are bundled together and offered at a discount. The preferred solutions create value for the customers by packaging products and services in ways that the customers cannot easily do for themselves.

Solutions therefore require an in-depth knowledge of the customer in order to identify the solutions that will be perceived as valuable and an ability to integrate product lines. In-depth customer knowledge is needed to identify the solutions that the customer will see as valuable. Then the supplier will need the ability to coordinate multiple profit centers from both inside and outside the company to create the value. Neither of these capabilities comes easily. Real estate agencies and banks have been searching for years for a mortgage solution for time-challenged home buyers that would combine the home loan, appraisal, title, title insurance, home insurance, and everything else into a single, sign-once package. Most of us are still waiting.

In addition to creating solutions, suppliers are trying to customize them. When everyone pursues the most profitable customers, they compete away the profits. One approach to holding onto valuable customers is to customize the solutions. Customization requires yet more in-depth knowledge of the customer and additional capability to integrate products and services into unique solutions.

So integral are solutions to the customer-centric capability that a large section of Chapter Two is devoted to an examination of the strategies necessary to achieve them.

Strategy and Organization Model

One of the primary barriers to converting to customer-centric organization is the belief that a company is already customer-centric when it is not. Most companies have spent the past twenty years getting closer to the customer using focus groups and measuring customer satisfaction. But just placing customers more prominently on the company's radar screen does not make the company customer-centric. That transition requires that the company literally organize around the customer. The next section defines what is meant by organization (it is more than structure) and then what is meant by a customer-centric organization. Readers can then judge for themselves how customer-centric their companies really are. They will then be able to judge how far their companies need to go in order to make the transition.

A model for linking different strategies to different organizations is shown in Figure 1.1 (Galbraith, 2002). It depicts an organization as consisting of five dimensions:

Figure 1.1 The Star Model

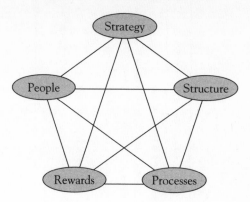

- Strategy, which determines direction
- Structure, which determines the location of decision-making power
- Processes, which have to do with the flow of information (they are the means of responding to information technologies)
- Reward systems, which influence the motivation of people to perform and address organizational goals
- People (human resource) policies, which influence and frequently define employees' mind-sets and skills

The message of the star model is that all five dimensions must be consistent among themselves, and the four below must be particularly consistent with strategy, at the top of the model. When the different combinations of organizational dimensions that characterize the more customer-centric capabilities are used, different solutions strategies can be identified and implemented.

Strategy

The differences begin with the elements that make up the strategy (Table 1.2). The product-centric company strives to have the best or leading products, achieved through a continuous flow of new

Table 1.2 Strategy: Product-Centric versus Customer-Centric

	Product-Centric Company	Customer-Centric Company
Strategy		
Goal	Best product for customer	Best solution for customer
Main offering	New products	Personalized packages of products, service, support, education, consulting
Value creation route	Cutting-edge products, useful features, new applications	Customizing for best total solution
Most important customer	Most advanced customer	Most profitable, loyal customer
Priority-setting basis	Portfolio of products	Portfolio of customers—customer profitability
Pricing	Price to market	Price for value, risk

offerings. The company remains at the cutting edge by adding new features that open the market to new applications and new customers. In contrast, the customer-centric company strives to provide the best solution for the customer's needs. This solution may or may not include the best products; the best solution will involve a customized and personalized package of reliable products, services, support, education, and consulting to make the customer more effective.

The most important customer for the product-centric company is the highly advanced customer. This customer challenges the company to stay on the cutting edge and develop new and improved products, which are priced on the basis of the market and competing offerings. The customer-centric company likes the advanced customer as well, but it is the most loyal and profitable customer that is the most important; the customer relationship is the valued asset. Based on this relationship, the customer-centric firm prices its offerings on the basis of the value it creates for the customer. That is, a solution is priced not on the sum of the prices of the products and services that constitute the solution, but on the savings and improvements that the customer experiences.

An example is the recent trend at business schools offering custom courses to companies. These courses were initially offered as products, like a one-week course in supply-chain management. For thirty to forty people, the price would be $150,000. If the company wanted customized cases and materials, it paid for the faculty time to develop these materials at $5,000 per faculty day. Now, instead of charging per week and per day, some schools are pricing to value. That is, they charge the company 5 percent of the savings that result from improvements to the supply chain generated by the program. If the company documents $100 million in savings, the school gets $5 million for the program. Value pricing shares the risks as well as the rewards: if there are no savings, the school gets nothing.

Pricing to value aligns the interests of the customer and the supplier. It also requires the supplier to have an in-depth knowledge of the customer's situation. In the example, the business school would need to know a great deal about supply-chain management and about the customer's unique version of supply. If the company were Unilever, the business school would need to know about frozen food supply chains as well as those that operate at ambient temperatures. This in-depth knowledge is best developed over time, through working relationships.

Structure and Processes

Decision making at the product-centric firm revolves around priority setting for a portfolio of products (Table 1.3). These decisions are facilitated by an organizational structure based on product line profit centers. The business plans and reviews are focused on products. When management reviews a business, the discussion is about products—competitors' products and new products. The entire orientation is different at the customer-centric company. The leaders there manage customer or customer segment profit centers. The plans, information systems, and business reviews revolve around customers; the company sets priorities around a portfolio of customers. These structures, conversations, and information systems shape the mind-sets of the leaders of these companies.

The management processes of planning and budgeting are oriented primarily around either products or customers. Likewise, the key business processes and measures of performance will be different. The most important process in a product-centric company is the new-product-development process; product-oriented companies like Sony and Hewlett-Packard devote a great deal of energy to designing and improving their processes for developing new products. The customer-centric company also develops products, but the most important processes are customer relationship management (CRM) and solutions development and product portfolio processes.

A customer-oriented company will invest heavily in a CRM process that captures customer interactions at all touch points for the most profitable customers. And in addition to a product development process, it will have a solutions development process to

Table 1.3 Structure and Processes: Product-Centric versus Customer-Centric

	Product-Centric Company	Customer-Centric Company
Structure	Organizational concept	Product profit centers, product reviews, product teams	Customer segments, customer teams, customer P&Ls
Processes	Most important process	New product development	Customer relationship management and solutions development

combine products and services to create value for the customers. Usually the customer-centric firm will invest along with partners in creating a replicable solutions platform when supplying a solution to the initial customer. And finally, a solutions provider must have a process for planning the entire product portfolio. Thus, when a computer company like IBM develops a new high-end server, it also needs a new high-end storage product to complement it. The software business needs to introduce a complementary operating system and an updated version of database software. Global services needs to introduce new courses from its education business, updated practice areas from its consulting and systems integration units, and new-customer service contracts. All of these business units need to have the same set of priorities. A storage business at a product-centric company would introduce the best product to exceed EMC's latest product. The companies therefore measure themselves differently: the product-centric company uses market share measures as well as targets for the percentage of revenue coming from new products; the customer-centric company measures success by the share of customer spending in the business area, as well as customer satisfaction and retention measures.

Rewards and People

The measures employed also become the basis for rewarding employees (Table 1.4). Product-centric companies reward salespeople and managers with commissions or bonuses based on market share, and technical people have as their highest reward being assigned to the most challenging next product. A customer-centric company like Siebel Systems uses commissions as well, but the commission is paid to the salesperson one year after the sale and is proportional to the customer's satisfaction with the software system purchased. (See Table 1.4.)

The most powerful people at a product-centric company are those who develop products. The product development function is the most powerful organizational unit, with people known by the

Table 1.4 Rewards and People: Product-Centric versus Customer-Centric

		Product-Centric Company	Customer-Centric Company
Rewards	Measures	• Number of new products • Percentage of revenue from products less than two years old • Market share	• Customer share of most valuable customer • Customer satisfaction • Lifetime value of a customer • Customer retention
People	Approach to personnel	Power to people who develop products • Highest reward is working on next most challenging product • Manage creative people through challenges with a deadline	Power to people with in-depth knowledge of customer's business • Highest rewards to relationship managers who save the customer's business
	Mental process	Divergent thinking: *How many possible uses of this product?*	Convergent thinking: *What combination of products is best for this customer?*
	Sales bias	On the side of the seller in a transaction	On the side of the buyer in a transaction
	Culture	New product culture: open to new ideas, experimentation	Relationship management culture: searching for more customer needs to satisfy

products they develop; everyone at 3M knows Art Fry and the story behind his development of Post-It Notes. Product-centric companies select and develop innovative types with in-depth product knowledge. The most powerful people at a customer-centric company are the re-lationship managers serving the most important customers. These companies work to develop general managers for an account, not salespeople for a product. The account managers have an in-depth knowledge of the customer and the customer's business and are skilled at building customer relationships. Whereas product-centric sales-people are transaction oriented, those who are customer-centric have relationship skill sets intended to generate repeat business.

Culture

All of these elements create a new-product culture or customer-re-lationship culture. While the mind-sets at product-centric compa-nies are focused on creating as many possible uses of the product as possible, customer-centric mind-sets search for the best combination of products for the customer and ways to expand the portion of the customer need set that they can serve. The greatest difference be-tween the two cultures is their allegiance in a transaction: a product-centric company like Sony is on the side of the seller, while the customer-centric consulting, systems integration, and outsourcing businesses at IBM are on the side of the buyer.

One corporation may find its subsidiaries on opposite sides of the culture. The branch personnel at Chase Manhattan Bank are on the side of the seller, promoting Chase credit cards and Chase mortgages for which they will receive a commission. But the relationship man-agers at Chase Private Bank (for their high-net-worth customers) are on the customer's side, suggesting the best investments—which may or may not be Chase mutual funds or the stocks issued by Chase's in-vestment bankers. The success of relationship managers is measured by customer satisfaction, retention, and asset growth.

Organizing around the customer involves adopting solutions strategies, customer profit centers, CRM processes, and customer-share and -retention reward systems and selecting and developing relationship managers. These practices create a relationship and a solutions culture.

A Word of Caution

It is possible to be customer-centric to a fault. For example Japanese software companies are usually accused of being dominated by their customers ("Breaking the Keiretsu," 2001). If a Japanese software company has two hundred customers, it will create two hundred versions of every software product that it offers. These companies have been unable to get scale and expand outside of Japan.

Another issue is becoming too focused on your best existing customers. New disruptive technologies are often adopted by different customers first (Christensen, 1997). Then as the technology improves, customers eventually move to the new disruptive technology. You lose your best customers because initially they were uninterested in the new technology. When they become interested, it is too late for you to change. Christensen's solution is to always have a unit prospecting for new customers and new technologies. When a possibly disruptive technology comes along, put it in a separate subsidiary and protect it from the core business. As always, a balanced perspective is needed.

Conclusion

With the advent of buyer power, the wise manager will be shifting the ramifications of "keep it simple" from an internal credo to a customer pledge. Companies should stop asking *if* a customer-centric application should be implemented, and instead ask *how much* customer-centricity is mandated to remain competitive and healthy.

The challenges facing implementation include discerning the appropriate level, taking the steps necessary for successful structural reorganization, and doing what is necessary for successful psychological reorientation. Unless the product-centric mind-set of personnel is updated along with the product-centric organization itself, no true growth can really be expected.

This chapter looked at organization. It consists of structure, business processes like CRM, management processes, reward systems, and human resource practices like selection. All of these areas are aligned around strategy. So when a company wants to become customer-centric, it means literally organizing around the customer. Table 1.1 gives a good idea of what a customer-centric organization looks like and how close or how far a company is from that model. The next chapter begins to address the issue of how customer-centric your organization should be. Not every company needs to adopt the extreme form of customer-centric organization.

2

CUSTOMER-CENTRICITY

How Much Is Enough?

In this chapter you will learn:

- That different solutions strategies require different levels of customer-centric organization.
- That solutions strategies vary in their scale and scope and integration requirements.
- How to determine your solutions strategy with the strategy locator.
- How to use the strategy locator to position your company on the customer-centric continuum.
- How to use lateral forms of organization to align the power and authority of your organization with your solutions strategy.

No two snowflakes or companies are the same. But while the strategic requirements of a snowflake are relatively simple—fall to the ground—those of a product-centric company are far more challenging. It could be said that in today's marketplace, specific and fundamental changes are necessary to prevent a company from falling to the ground, and because no two companies are the same, a one-size-fits-all application is not the answer.

This chapter discusses how to determine the level of customer-centricity necessary for your company. It begins by describing the different kinds of customer relationship strategies, from which will be determined the level of customer-centricity to be implemented.

Customer Relationship Strategies

A number of authors, using slightly different wording, have argued the case for becoming customer-centric (Day, 1990, 1999; Vandermerve, 1999; Wiersema, 1998; Peppers and Rogers, 1997, 2001; Selden and Colvin, 2003), and have described the details of a customer relationship strategy. They make several points that need to be underlined here.

First, many customers want relationships with key suppliers. Although companies are using auctions and reverse auctions to purchase commodities, they are choosing a few long-term suppliers for their unique requirements.

Second, customers want close relationships through which they can engage in dialogue with suppliers for the purpose of detailing their customization desires.

Third, these dialogues create opportunities for astute suppliers to discover unmet customer needs and requirements, and can then expand their offerings to include more products and services. More important, these suppliers can develop packages of products and services that create value for customers. These packages or solutions make the customer more effective, and the more effective the customer feels as a result, the more the customer will engage in dialogue with and use the supplier. A virtuous circle can result.

Following this prescription to establish a relationship ultimately leads a corporation to offer more than stand-alone products; it leads it to offering solutions. Let us look at several solutions strategies that will determine the level of customer-centricity.

Strategic Choice

The different types of solutions described here will guide the choice of organization to implement that strategy. But first there must be the conscious choice of a customer relationship strategy for the company. The contrast between Nestlé and Procter & Gamble is illuminating. Both are consumer packaged goods manufacturers delivering a large number of products to the same retail customers. On our strategy locator (described later in this chapter), both would measure 5 on the scale and scope dimension. Yet Nestlé has chosen to remain a product-centric company and uses informal processes only to coordinate account management around the large, global retailers. P&G, in contrast, has chosen to focus on these retailers and form global supply-chain partnerships. Some retailers, like Wal-Mart, even outsource the management of product categories and aisles to them. So a company still needs to do its strategy homework to decide whether becoming customer-centric will be an advantage for it.

In other industries, gaining customer-centricity is becoming a necessity. Both Hewlett-Packard and Motorola saw that the digital revolution held out opportunities too good to pass by. Currently, almost all product-centric consumer electronics companies, like Sony and Philips, are experiencing the digital pull to provide solutions. In the automotive industry, the tier I suppliers to the auto original equipment manufacturers (OEM) are finding themselves faced with a few very large customers. For those in tier I, becoming customer-centric is less of a choice and more of a necessity. (The automotive supply chain is led by the OEMs like General Motors and Toyota. They are supplied by the tier I suppliers, which are supplied in turn by the tier II suppliers, and so on.)

The points here are that there are industry- and company-specific factors that must be weighed when choosing whether to implement customer relationship strategies. However, in many—if not most—industries, these factors are leading companies to become more customer-centric and to offer solutions. The following types of solutions strategies will help to determine how customer-centric you need to become.

Different Types of Solutions

Companies that follow a relationship strategy that leads to solutions bundle their products together and add software and services. These packages create more value than the customers can create for themselves by buying only the stand-alone products. For the customer, solutions constitute a limited form of outsourcing, which allows them to focus on their core business. For the suppliers, solutions constitute an alternative to products that commoditize rapidly. The challenge to the supplier is to create an organization that can package and deliver the solutions.

The organization that can deliver these solutions is one that fits with the solutions strategy. There are four dimensions of solutions strategy—two major and two minor—that appear to make a difference to the organization. The major dimensions are the scale and scope of solutions and the degree of integration of products and services; the minor dimensions are the types of solutions and the percentage of total revenue deriving from solutions.

Scale and Scope.   The first major strategic factor having a great organizational impact is the scale and scope of the solution. *Scale* and *scope* refer to the number of products and the number of different kinds of products that are combined into a solution. For example, a small-scale and -scope solution would be a local area network for a work group. A dozen desktop computers, a shared printer, and disk storage could all be linked by an ethernet cable and form a network.

A larger-scale and -scope solution would be computer-aided design (CAD) system for an engineering department of several hundred engineers. This solution would require desktops, servers, storage units, CAD software, database software, network software, and installation and maintenance services. It may also require financing and training of the engineers. This CAD solution comprises many more products and many different kinds of products—software and services as well as hardware products.

At the extreme end of scale and scope, Mitsubishi Trading Company could order state-of-the-art trading floors for ten thousand traders at six worldwide sites. This solution requires hardware, software, and services for computers, telecom, financing, and training. Large turnkey projects such as these are an extreme challenge to organization design and require a highly integrated approach.

Integration. The second major dimension is the degree of integration between the components that comprise a solution. Integration varies from a loose assortment of products to a highly integrated combination. In between are combinations that use modular architectures. Little integration is needed between products supplied by agriculture firms to farmers. The firms try to bundle seeds, herbicides, insecticides, and consulting. However, the farmer can easily buy each as a stand-alone product from a different supplier.

An example of larger-scale but still limited integration can be found at ISS in Europe and ARAMARK and ServiceMaster in the United States. They try to provide as many simple services as possible, with one-stop shopping for security, catering, janitorial, parking lot management, landscaping, building maintenance, and many other similar services. But each is a relatively independent service that could be provided by an independent service company. A more integrated offering is the set of solutions from computer companies. Figure 2.1 shows what Sun Microsystems calls the integrated stack. The stack shows hardware on the bottom, software in the middle, and services on the top.

All hardware and software components have to operate in an integrated manner. (The services are somewhat more independent.) But thanks to standards like the Java programming language, components using Java can be substituted for other components. For example, a customer could choose BEA's middleware or IBM's Websphere and substitute it for Sun's i-Planet middleware. Therefore, components in the information technology industry must be able to operate with other-branded components; by following standards, the customer has the choice of mixing and matching.

At the extreme are integral solutions in which the components are unique but are designed specifically to work together. A simple integral solution would be an antilock braking system (ABS) for an auto manufacturer. Each ABS is unique to an automobile model. Johnson Controls is a more complex example. The company designs and manufactures interiors for Toyota, Chrysler, and other automobile OEMs. Each Toyota model has a unique interior comprising

Figure 2.1 Sun's Integrated Stack

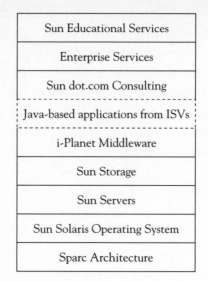

Note: The dashed lines signify that there may be more than one application.

unique parts; these parts cannot be used on a Chrysler interior. The significance of the integration dimension for the organization is the coordination required. The organization reflects the solution. The more interdependent the components are, the more interdependent are the organizational units responsible for those components and the larger the challenge is to rapidly mobilize them.

The combination of scale and scope with integration determines the coordination requirements and the organizational features to provide the necessary coordination. Figure 2.2 shows this combination and some different solutions strategies that have been discussed.

Figure 2.2 shows that scale and scope and integration increase as the solutions move from the lower-left to the upper-right corner. The consequence is that the coordination requirements increase in the same manner. We will focus first on the low levels and then examine the medium and then the more complex solutions and customer-centric organizations.

Figure 2.2   Coordination Requirements of Different Solutions Strategies

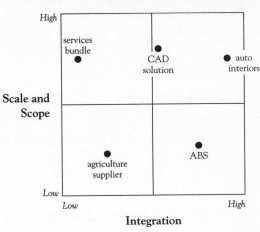

Types of Solutions.   There are two main types of solutions: horizontal and vertical. Horizontal solutions are generic and apply across customer categories. For example, Sun Microsystems creates and delivers a human resource portal solution that can be used for the human resource function across all industries. IBM also delivers industry-specific solutions. For example, e-Agency is a solution to put the agency network of an insurance company on the Internet. These industry-specific solutions are referred to as vertical solutions. Clearly, the vertical solutions require a more customer-centric organizational unit than do the horizontal solutions.

Revenues.   The last strategic dimension is the percentage of total revenues that comes from solutions. If, like Motorola, solutions contribute 10 percent or less, the firm can simply add a solutions unit whose task is to integrate the firm's products into solutions. When the percentage gets higher, as at IBM, the company has sufficient volume to specialize the solutions units that serve different customer segments. Instead of one solutions unit, IBM has about twelve, each specializing in a customer segment as several in global services for the generic horizontal solutions.

The Provider Challenges. In summary, a solutions provider desiring to respond quickly to customer opportunities faces greater challenges as its strategy increases in the scale and scope of the solution provided and the degree of integration of the components comprising the solution.

Scale and scope increase the number of organizational units that must be integrated quickly. Integration relates to the coordination effort needed to accomplish the requisite integration. In combination, these two factors determine the amount of customer centricity that is needed and the strength of customer-facing organizational units.

The Strategy Locator

Now that customer relationship strategies have been defined and detailed, it is time to determine your specific company's requirements in these areas.

Of utmost importance to your company is the level of customer-centricity that it should implement. Too little or too much could prove significantly counterproductive, so ascertaining the proper level is key.

The following lists have been compiled to help you determine the level—low, medium, or high—that will give your corporation or division optimal performance. Locate your company on each of the lists for scale and scope and for integration. Pick the location on the list that best describes the offerings of your company or division.

Scale and Scope

- My company has two to five similar products or services to sell to the same customer.
- We offer five to ten mostly products and services.
- We have ten to fifteen products or services of different types to sell to the same customer.
- We have fifteen to twenty variegated products or services to sell to the same customer.

- We have more than twenty products or services of various different types to sell to the same customer.

Integration

- My company provides stand-alone products to the same customer with common invoice and billing ("one-stop shopping").
- We have a set of minimally connected stand-alone products (like a common brand, common experience, combined shipment).
- We have minimally packaged (themed) components that need to work together for customer segments.
- We have modular components of products and services that need to work tightly together as a system.
- We have very tightly integrated packages/bundles/full solutions of products and services to offer the customer.

If your total from both lists is one to three, then you will benefit most from the information for the light-level implementation of the customer-centric application. Locations on the two lists totaling four to seven would require the midlevel implementation of the application. A total of eight to ten means that your corporation will gain the most benefit from the full, strong-level implementation of customer-centricity. (Figure 2.3 illustrates your score. This model is used throughout the book to show other companies.)

Chapter Three begins the process of actual implementation for the company falling into the light-level category. This information will be supplemented in Chapter Four with the additional information necessary for the midlevel application. If yours is a complete-level company, you will require the full cumulative information of Chapters Three through Eight.

Creating a Lateral Networking Capability

In order to implement a responsive customer-centric capability, companies also need a lateral networking capability. Because they

Figure 2.3 Customer-Centric Strategy Locator

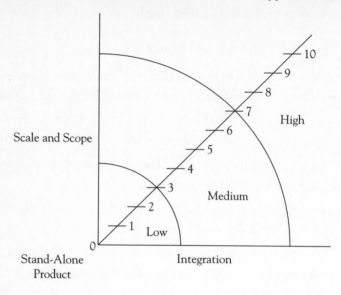

have been organized by business units, countries, and functions, organizing around the customer requires that they create networks across these dimensions.

To create multiproduct solutions for global customers, a company must work through lateral networks. A simple company with a few local customers selling a single product can work through a functional hierarchy. But a company with multiple product lines in multiple countries using multiple functions must work less through hierarchy and more through networks. Indeed, a company needs a network for each strategically important dimension. Some companies, like Philips, have organized around global product lines called business units. They have created country and functional networks to coordinate across product lines. Other companies, like Nestlé, have organized around country and regional profit centers. They have created product (called strategic business units) and functional networks to coordinate across their geographical structure.

There are different kinds of networks, and the organization design challenge is to match the right kind of network with the strategic importance of the customer dimension. Some networks are informal, and others are formal with varying degrees of strength. These formal networks vary in power and in the cost to coordinate across the other dimensions. A list of these networks is shown in Figure 2.4. This is an ordered list, with the simplest, cheapest, and easiest to use listed first. The further up the list, the more powerful the networks—and the more costly and difficult to employ them. The designer should start at the bottom of the list and proceed up until a network is found that matches the coordination requirements of the customer dimension for their business. This list corresponds to the score on the strategy locator. The bottom of the lateral forms is for stand-alone products and the top for highly complex solutions. The low and medium levels of complexity require increasingly more powerful forms of lateral returnables.

Informal Networks and E-Coordination

Informal or voluntary networks form naturally in all organizations. Management, however, can initiate them and then let them proceed under their own energy. Nestlé is an example, with informal networks that have formed around global customers. Although Nestlé, unlike a corporation such as Procter & Gamble, has not strategically focused on cross-border customers like Carrefour or Wal-Mart, the Nestlé country managers and country account managers for Wal-Mart routinely exchange information and ideas about the global retailers on an informal basis.

This informal exchange was judged to be sufficient until the Internet allowed more formal communication (while still maintaining informal coordination). Now the country manager in the headquarters country of the global customer maintains a database about that customer and issues e-mails and updates about the customer. Anyone dealing with the customer can add information and

Figure 2.4 Types of Networks for Customer-Facing Units

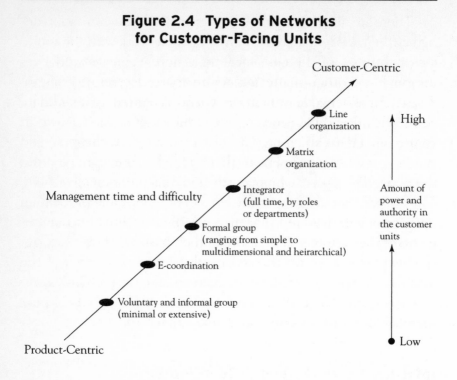

ideas. But this is still an informal network: each country treats the information as an input and then acts in the best interest of its product lines and country profit and loss statement (P&L). This form is called e-coordination in Figure 2.4.

More intensive and more formal versions of e-coordination can be used. (A version will be illustrated by an investment bank in Chapter Four.) The formal communication among all people interacting with customers is the approach taken by companies, such as the investment bank, wanting to show one face to the customer. Each contact is recorded and entered into a database. Others can see this running record when they deal with the customer. Each person then deals with the customer according to function but records all information, to be used across functions. This electronic coordination is a slight increase in the cost and effort to coordinate across units for the customer.

Formal Teams

Formal teams are the next level of strength that can be applied to a customer network, usually implemented when a customer desires more than informal coordination. Citibank started with teams for a few accounts and expanded them to over 450 within a few years to accommodate all customers that wanted a coordinated cross-border service. An example of this level is the formation of global or key account teams, which are created by appointing all of a customer's sales and account representatives to an account team for that customer. These representatives, from all product lines and all countries, exchange information, as the Nestlé informal networks do, but also meet regularly, prepare an account plan, and agree on customer-specific goals. The account manager in the customer's home country usually leads the team, which consists of a few core members and a larger extended team to encompass the salespeople from every customer location.

The customer teams can be strengthened and assume more activities when customers want partnerships along the supply chain. Wal-Mart and P&G provide an example. P&G initially formed a team of its salespeople that represented all products that P&G provided to Wal-Mart. The team was expanded to include manufacturing, distribution, marketing, information technology, and finance. This team of about eighty people, representing various functions from all product lines, worked to synchronize the product and order flow from P&G factories to Wal-Mart warehouses to minimize inventories and cut cycle times. Today, as Wal-Mart expands globally, this team consists of 250 people from different functions, product lines, and countries.

Degussa Automotive Catalysts takes the team one step further, including research and development (R&D) participation. Degussa salespeople serve DaimlerChrysler by coordinating across borders (like the lower-complexity Citibank application does) and also partnering along the supply chain to synchronize their production with the DaimlerChrysler assembly lines (as Procter & Gamble does with Wal-Mart). In addition, Degussa engineers determine DaimlerChrysler's new-product needs and coordinate with the auto-maker on creating new catalysts for new engines on Daimler's automotive platforms. Degussa creates customer-specific, engine-specific, and platform-specific catalysts for exhaust emissions. Its formal team structure is described and analyzed in Chapter Three as an example of the low level of customer-centricity and solutions complexity.

Formal customer networks can therefore vary from a few key account teams for salespeople; to supply-chain-partnership teams of sales, logistics, and other functional people; to new-product-development teams that represent all functions, including the various engineering functions.

For companies like Degussa, this customer team organization is sufficient to meet the needs of its most important customer. Other companies, like Citibank, take the further step of creating a full-time coordinator to manage all of the customer team activities.

Integrator

The next step to move the customer dimension to a more powerful position is creating a coordinator for key accounts. When a company creates fifty or more teams and the customer wants still more coordination, the key account or global account coordinator role is a useful addition to the informal networks and formal customer teams.

The coordinator provides two new factors. First, the coordinator becomes a voice for the customer on the management team, which usually consists of managers of product lines, geographies, and functions. The coordinator gets the leadership thinking in terms of a portfolio of customers, customer priorities, and customer-centricity. Customer teams can also appeal to the coordinator in resolving conflicts. The teams can solicit a high-level voice to defend them in conflicts with more product-centric parts of the company.

The second task of the coordinator is building and managing the infrastructure that supports customer teams. The coordinator assumes the role of managing customer information systems and communications across customer teams. The coordinator usually creates training programs for managers and team members regarding the role and operation of key accounts. Many coordinators create a common planning system for customer plans: fifty customer teams are likely to create fifty planning formats, and the coordinator agrees on a single, common one.

Another key addition to the infrastructure is a customer accounting system, which leads to customer P&Ls—customer profitability is a key measure in setting customer priorities. Asymmetries in costs and revenues always occur across geographies. The customer account manager and team in the customer's home country expend extra effort to make a sale to their customer. Often the initiative is successful, but the customer's first purchases are for its subsidiaries in other countries. Thus, the costs are incurred in the home country, but revenues are booked in other countries. A global accounting system for customers can identify these asymmetries, and management can correct for them. When companies like Citibank expand to over 450 teams, the network coordinator is often expanded into a network coordination department. At Citi, the 450 customers were organized into industry-specific units, and a network coordinator was appointed for each industry group.

All of these infrastructure additions can be combined in the planning process. The countries and product lines can set customer-specific goals for key accounts, and then customer teams, countries, and product lines will pursue an aligned set of goals.

When a higher level of organization is required to coordinate the countries and product lines, a further step up the lateral organization ladder may be chosen.

Matrix Organization

The next step to enhance the power base of the customer dimension is the formation of units within countries and product lines that are dedicated to customers, customer segments, or industries and report to the network coordinator for the customer unit. In countries where the company may not control 100 percent of the equity, joint ventures that serve multinational clients are often created between the parent company and the local subsidiary.

The assumption here is that the customer dimension has attained a strategic importance equal to the countries or business units. This importance is expressed by making the customer organization an equal partner in the decision-making process.

When the customer needs still more prominence in the organizational structure, there is one more complexity that may be added.

Separate Customer Line Organization

The final step is to create a separate customer-facing structure by gathering all dedicated customer-specific resources from the product lines, countries, and functions. Companies serving the automotive customer like Johnson Controls have formed customer business units (CBUs). Companies like IBM form customer segment profit centers by gathering all relationship managers into industry groups. These industry groups call on product profit centers for additional staffing as the opportunities require. They are usually profit centers themselves and are measured on customer profitability. These separate customer-facing units are the most powerful—and most customer-centric—form of organizing around the customer.

Matching Organizational Units and Solutions Strategy

The important point of this chapter is that the level of power and authority vested in the customer-centric organizational units should match the level of solutions strategy. As a company introduces a low-solutions strategy, it should use a level of lateral forms such as formal teams (as will be demonstrated in Chapter Three, with the example of Degussa). When it chooses a medium level of solutions strategy, it should include a higher level of coordination, such as a network coordinator, in addition to the informal lateral forms (as

Figure 2.5 Matching Strategy Location to Lateral Coordination Requirements

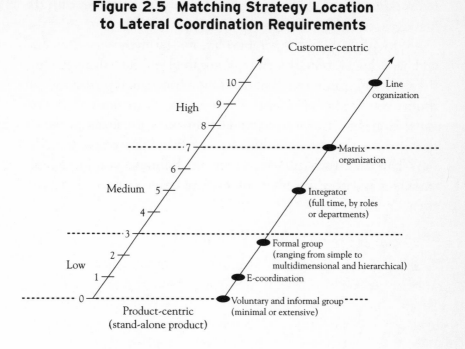

will be illustrated by the investment bank example in Chapter Four). Finally, the high level of solutions strategy requires a separate customer unit to achieve the necessary level of customer-centricity. Chapter Five illustrates IBM's organization to implement its high-complexity solutions strategy. Thus, the choice of type of strategy shown in Figure 2.4 should be matched by the strength of the customer organizational form shown in Figure 2.5.

Conclusion

An essential tool for implementing the application is lateral networking capability, which can be delineated in five cumulative levels of complexity.

The art of the implementation process comes from discerning the appropriate amount of the customer-centric application and choosing the requisite solutions and a corresponding level of lateral network complexity. The next chapter begins this process with the first steps, referred to as light-level application.

In this chapter, the different solutions strategies were described and placed on a strategy locator. You can locate your strategy using the strategy locator and then determine how much power and authority you need to allocate to the customer dimensions of your organization. Lateral forms were described as the means by which power and authority can be aligned with the strategy locator. In the next chapters, examples are given for light- to complete-level strategies and how the companies aligned their organizations with their strategies.

3

Light-Level Application

In this chapter you will learn:

- How to apply the strategy locator to the light version of a customer-centric strategy.

- How to use customer teams as the structural form for the light strategy.

- How to implement the total organization design by using management processes, measures, rewards, and people practices to complement the strategy and structure.

- That the leadership is the key ingredient for putting all of the pieces together.

The range of options for implementing degree of customer-centricity is less a definitive choice from three sizes and more a determined point on a continuum of complexity. For expediency, the options seem to be divided here into the static checkpoints of low, medium, and high, but these should rather be considered the delineations of chunks of the continuum; a company requiring low-level application will place itself somewhere along the first chunk, a medium-level application will fall within the middle chunk, and a high-level application will be situated in the high-end chunk.

Customer Lite

This chapter focuses on a company that has incorporated a "lite" version of the customer relationship and the customer-centric organization (the first chunk). I have used Nestlé as an example of a product-centric company whose customer-focused organization was an informal one (which more recently became Internet based). Degussa's Catalytic Converter division has formulated a stronger customer relationship strategy and has implemented it using customer teams. Degussa has implemented a more customer-centric strategy, though it measures only a 3 on the strategy locator score. This customer strategy has evolved because of its extensive interaction with its auto OEM customer in customizing unique products for them. Also, Degussa is dealing with a few strong auto OEMs that know how to use buying power. (Nestlé watches global retailers like Wal-Mart and Carrefour carefully but sells into a much less concentrated market.) And finally Degussa participates in the supply of an integrated auto exhaust system solution while providing one of the components. It actively participates in the design of the exhaust systems by partnering with the engine group at the auto OEM, the electronic engine controls supplier (such as Bosch), and the assembler of the tailpipe, muffler, and catalytic converter system.

In terms of the framework being developed here, Degussa is shown in Figure 3.1. The company is depicted as low on the solutions strategy locator. Its low position results from measuring 1 on scale and scope and 2 on integration. The 2 results from its supply chain partnership integration. Degussa uses formal teams as well as informal contacts to become more customer-centric than Nestlé.

Degussa Automotive Catalysts Division

Degussa AG (which was recently acquired by the OM Group) places a specialized chemical formulation including platinum and palladium catalysts on substrate pieces, which are inserted into automotive exhaust systems by the tier I assembler. The catalyst pro-

Figure 3.1 Low Solutions Complexity
Uses Formal Teams

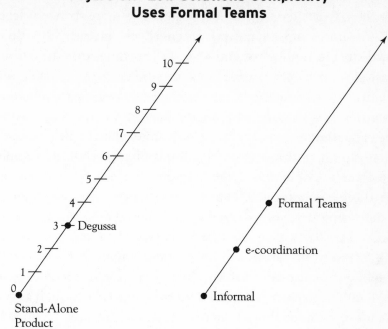

Note: The right figure shows the lateral forms that Degussa used.

motes a chemical reaction to reduce harmful emissions from tailpipe exhaust. It is a tier II supplier but a tier I developer to the automotive OEMs like BMW and Volkswagen. The development role is the driver of organizing around the OEM automotive customer.

The division has revenues of 600 million euros, half of which is the catalysts for the OEMs. The rest is supplying precious metals. It started in the auto catalysts business in 1974 and by 1980 had a 4 percent global market share. Today it has a 20 percent share, which is increasing because of its technology. Degussa has factories in Germany, the United States (joint venture, JV), Canada, Mexico, Korea (JV), Japan (JV), South Africa (JV), Brazil (JV), and Thailand and is considering starting up in India, China (JV), Argentina, and Sweden.

The business opportunity is driven by the reduction of exhaust emissions, largely because of legislation. The more stringent legislation requires more catalysts. Degussa sees growth because of growth in the number of autos, growth in miles driven, and increasing populations in urban areas around the world. Also it sees opportunity in diesel fuels, which have superior thermodynamic properties. It is working with engine designers at the OEMs to reduce exhaust emissions, the negative feature of diesel fuel. Fuel cells are another opportunity. A fuel cell is itself a catalyst of platinum on carbon black plus four other different catalysts. So Degussa supplies three basic products: catalysts for standard engines, catalysts for diesel engines, and eventually fuel cells. These three give it a score of 1 on the scale and scope dimension of strategy.

Degussa works directly with the design engineers in the engine component of the auto OEM. Once a vendor is selected by an OEM and its product is designed into the auto platform, it is very difficult to dislodge the supplier. The product must be certified by the government and the OEM. Each catalyst is specific to an engine and a platform. Once it is designed in, the OEM does not change it for the life of the vehicle. The product can be subject to recall. If an OEM designs in a catalyst that is reliable, it is reluctant to change the equipment. So the competition is to get in early, like India, when legislation is being enacted to control emissions.

Competitive advantage comes from a solid chemical background and skill in handling and know-how of precious metals. Platinum and palladium are subject to global supply movements and speculation. The production process requires precise control. It is the micrograms of platinum that make the difference between profit and loss. AlliedSignal entered the business on the basis of its competence in chemical catalysts. However, it never mastered the handling of the precious metals and did not control supply of the material. It sold the business to Delphi.

The business is a regulation- and technology-driven enterprise where the most sophisticated and demanding customer is the European OEM. European drivers demand high-performing engines, and strong green political parties are demanding stringent pollution controls. Degussa's technical superiority has led to a 25 percent annual growth rate. The industry demand grows at only 5 to 6 percent per year. So Degussa has used its technology and relationship with the OEMs to increase market share.

Organization

The leadership of Degussa's Automotive Catalysts Division believes that its organization is one of its sources of competitive advantage. It has a formal structure like many other companies and an extensive lateral organization. One of the lateral structures is built around customer teams. The formal structure is shown in Figure 3.2.

Until recently, the division was a functional structure, appropriate for a single business. Then the sales and marketing function was divided into three geographical business units for the Americas, Europe and South Africa (the main source of platinum), and

Figure 3.2 Automotive Catalysts Division Structure

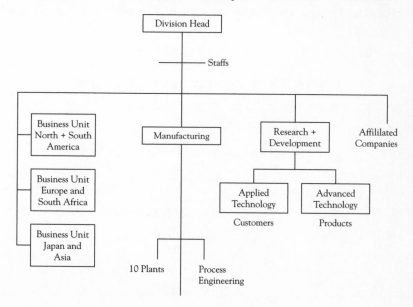

Japan and the rest of Asia. The change represents Degussa's increasing global presence and priority given to emerging markets. The functions of manufacturing and R&D remain the same but are matrixed across the new business units.

A key lateral organization is the customer team. There is one team for each major OEM with which the division works. The customer team structure is shown in Figure 3.3.

The customer is at the top of the structure. The layer between the customer and the executive committee is the customer business team. The executive committee consists of the division manager, the three business unit managers, and the manufacturing and R&D functional managers. Each customer team has a coach who is a member of the executive committee. The purpose is to allow rapid escalation of issues to the executive committee. Platinum catalysts are a volatile product from politically sensitive places like Russia and South Africa. Platinum itself can be price volatile and subject to speculation. It can require priority setting around customers and plants. Since platinum is a very high-value ingredient, it influences value-added statistics that governments watch. It is subject to changes in value-added legislation, import duties, and subsidies. A change in these factors will cause a customer to shift its source of supply from

Figure 3.3 Customer Team Structure

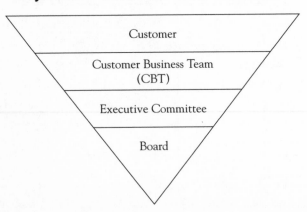

Brazil to South Africa. So Degussa maintains a portfolio of producing sites and the flexibility to move production among those sites.

Another factor is pricing. The teams coordinate prices for Volkswagen worldwide. The price for Volkswagen in Germany must be coordinated with prices for Volkswagen in Brazil, China, and Mexico. Prices are adjusted for shipping, imports, duties, and taxes. The price is not identical but must be coordinated for all customer locations.

The third purpose of the customer team is to coordinate the design of the new products for new customer platforms. Degussa wants to get close to the customers in order to get ahead of the competitors. It wants to be able to anticipate the customer requirements and therefore needs to know customer engine requirements three to five years in advance. It has a resident engineer or engineers at the customer site to learn about what is going on there. These resident engineers relay information to R&D. When a lead is discovered, R&D starts searching for solutions, which may involve exotic chemicals like rare earths, and explores environmental impacts, resource availability, costs, and other factors. It tries to be better organized than competitors on these issues. The goal is to be ahead of the customer and competitors. By knowing first and knowing better, Degussa can prepare and move ahead. Then when the customer's management comes to Degussa, it already has a project team in place and a set of alternatives prepared. When successful, it can even influence the customer's preferences.

A customer team is a form of matrix organization. The structure shown in Figure 3.4 is a combination of countries and functions. It consists of core team members and extended team members. The core team consists of the sales and marketing representatives from each country in which the customer is present and makes buying decisions. They are in contact with the customer every day. Other core team members are functional representatives from the country in which the customer is based. The decision center for the customer is in the home country. The team leader can come from the applied technology function, which is itself organized by customer. The sales and marketing representative could also be the team

Figure 3.4 Volkswagen Customer Team

	Brazil	Germany	North America	China
Marketing and Sales	X	X	X	X
Applied Technology		LEADER		
R&D		X		
Manufacturing	V	X	V	V
Logistics		X		
Quality		X		

X = member of core team; V = member of extended team

leader. In the customer's home country, the applied technology engineer and the sales and marketing representative are 100 percent dedicated to the customer. The extended team members are functional representatives from other countries in which the customer is present. They become active when building or adding to a plant, introducing a new product, or creating the business plan.

Business planning is done by the customer and the customer business team. The teams prepare a plan for each customer engine by engine, process by process, country by country, and function by function. They make a list of all future opportunities and a list of problem areas. Degussa stresses the norm of not hiding problems. Problems are to be solved, not lead to punishment. Priorities are set and programs are initiated or continued. These plans are reviewed and updated quarterly in relation to goals, milestones, and strategies. The teams are measured by customer share.

Degussa's customer teams were started five years ago with one team for Daimler-Benz. The Degussa salespeople were initially worried; they felt that they owned the customer relationship. But as problems were solved, people began to see the benefits and to enjoy the teamwork. The cost was time taken from functional jobs. Other teams were added. The company has always experimented with teams. For example, it has tried electing team leaders and rotating the leader role and has finally settled on selection by the executive committee. The leader role is now evaluated higher, and people want the opportunity to hold this position.

Currently there is concern about some competition between the customer teams. Degussa has always allowed some competition between teams. Sometimes the request comes from the customers. Currently there are two dedicated teams working on fuel injection projects for different customers. The two teams are developing different catalysts for the same application. Both have signed nondisclosure agreements. The leaders of the teams stay informed. They will prevent failures but will allow different solutions. When not restricted, these leaders are the links between teams and the means of spreading best practices. The executive committee had a meeting and discussion with the team leaders about the current situation in general. It is discussing what steps to take to maintain a balance. So the leadership is constantly monitoring and improving the performance of the team process.

Another formal meeting is the Automotive Catalyst Steering Committee, which meets twice annually and consists of the executive committee and the general managers of the major subsidiaries around the world. The purposes of the meeting are to deal with customer and capacity issues, transfer ideas, and increase local capabilities. There is a continuous upgrading of manufacturing processes. Since Degussa tries to maintain similar equipment in all plants, it starts a process in one plant and then expands it around the world. Most recently, Brazil was the transmitter or lead plant. The start-up of the process is carried out by the transmitter and is assisted by teams from the subsequent receiving plants. Canada, South Africa, and Germany all assisted in the start-up of the process in Brazil. The steering committee addresses cross-country, cross-customer-capacity issues.

Other Lateral Organizational Forms

The manufacturing function meets once a year and focuses on benchmarking. There are common and extensive measures for all ten facilities. These are sent out on CD-ROMs monthly showing all measures for all plants, with reports by process and by customer. At the initial meetings, there was consternation about comparative measures. In response, the leadership tried to reduce defensiveness by setting norms and explaining that the measures provided an opportunity to talk and learn. They were not to be a punishment or an embarrassment for those that did not seem to measure up. Another step was to push the discussion to the detail level and continually ask why there were differences. They also use measures to show rates of improvement. (Usually the lowest performer is the top improver.) Degussa encourages visits and other exchanges across the plants. The goal is to get people to travel and move around the world and create an effective network.

Traditionally, the interface between R&D and manufacturing has been a tension point. Degussa's Catalyst Division has worked to make sure that both units are aware of the other's problems and appreciate the issues. They hold regular workshops at which both groups are in attendance and the focus is on product teams and new-product programs. In addition, there are rotational assignments across the interface, people are colocated in each other's department areas, and they work with each other on the customer and new-product teams.

Today teams are formed without executive committee involvement. R&D and applied technology are an example. R&D is organized by product and applied technology by customer. Applied technology is then also organized into liaison groups to link better with R&D. The purpose is to speed the transfer of ideas and improve cooperation on new-product programs. Product life cycles are speeding up, with a generation appearing every year or two. There are more new products, so this interface is crucial.

Another series of lateral forms takes place around the Total Quality Management (TQM) initiative, which was started in the early 1990s to tear down organizational barriers. There had been several attempts at TQM in the past, and many people had been through Crosby training, a popular Total Quality program. At one point there were more projects than people in the division. The effort then began anew, with the result that there are no more than five projects at any one time. The projects are chosen by the TQM steering committee, which is chaired by a member of the executive committee. The members range from the general manager of the division to the operators from the factories. The operators rotate through the committee. Initially those who resisted were identified and placed on the committee. They have since become converts.

The TQM steering committee holds workshops for training and problem surfacing. Usually these are cross-departmental process meetings, with some members of the executive committee in attendance.

The meetings are held in a hotel overnight. The intent is to have people mix, get to know others informally, and socialize together. The meetings are a forum to teach the business to the employees and to listen to what the people believe are the issues. The meetings result in projects to improve standard business processes. One such project is to introduce new products faster so that more can be launched.

Overall Degussa has an extensive lateral organization (Figure 3.5). The key team is the customer team, but there are also product teams, process teams at transmitting factories, functional teams and meetings, and TQM process project teams. The product teams are subteams to the customer teams. Priorities and conflicts encountered in these teams can be quickly escalated to steering committees or the executive committee, whose members stay involved so that they can stay informed and quickly resolve these issues.

Figure 3.5 Team Structure

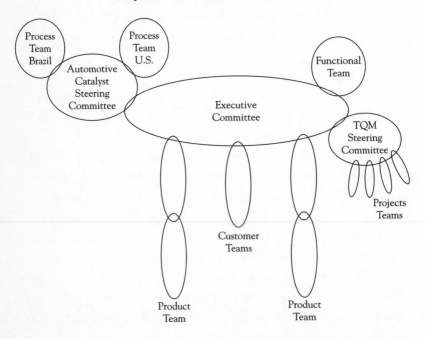

Measures and Reward Systems

The key process is the planning process, which takes place around customers and is created by the customer teams. These result in programs for the teams and in goals and milestones for the team members. The teams were measured on the share of the customer's business that they win.

The plans and the actual performance of the customer teams are added up for the regional business units (RBUs), which are then measured on the basis of a measure similar to earnings before interest and taxes for each OEM that is headquartered in the region. Figure 3.6 illustrates the situation.

The RBU manager for the Americas is measured on the global profitability of General Motors and Ford. So revenues and costs, no matter where they accrue, are assigned to customers' accounts. The RBU manager for Europe is responsible for the global profitability of Volkswagen, DaimlerChrysler, Renault, and others. The RBUs are not just regional entities but are globally responsible for their locally headquartered customers. The customer team leaders also have

Figure 3.6. Regional Business Unit Customer Measurement

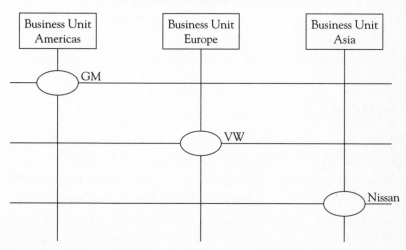

an allegiance to the RBU manager as well as to their function. The country managers of the subsidiaries are still measured on a country P&L. They serve all customers in their countries. These measures add a constant tension to the country-region relation. They both have a different view.

The other processes are the order fulfillment process and the new-product-development process. Both have been the subject of redesign efforts in the auto industry. At Degussa they are also the subject of continual improvements and projects in the TQM initiative. All of Degussa's plants carry certifications like ISO 9000, QS 9000, UDA 6.1, and ISO 14000, respectively. The new-product-development process in particular was singled out in the earlier discussion of improving the interfaces between R&D, applied technology, and manufacturing.

The new-product-development process also includes alliances with other partners. An example of a current one involves Daimler-Chrysler and Bosch. Daimler is designing a new diesel engine, and Bosch is simultaneously developing the electronic engine control system. On this project, Degussa is simultaneously designing a new catalyst to reduce exhaust emissions. The project involves controlling not only the engine temperature but also the catalyst temperature. A constant temperature at the catalyst-exhaust surface leads to more complete reactions and fewer emissions. It is necessary for all three components to be designed simultaneously. A dedicated team from the three partners is conducting the design effort using the Daimler product development process.

Information Technology

Degussa claims not to be a trendsetter in electronic communications. Earlier I noted that it sends a monthly CD-ROM and quarterly reports to factories and encourages travel. Today it is increasing the use of e-mail and videoconferencing and is making an effort to increase the use of Lotus Notes. On Lotus Notes it has folders for each customer and competitor. The folder for VW, for example, lists all contacts and which catalyst products VW uses, maintains a customer database, and lists the latest call reports and competitive information. All benchmarking data are being placed on the Notes program. With a collaborative culture in place, the electronic links should be easier to implement.

Human Resource Processes

Degussa's HR processes are geared around selecting, developing, and rewarding those people who can work within the TQM value system. The hiring process is selective and seeks people who can work without a hierarchy. The process uses a realistic job preview and peer interviewing. When Degussa's CEO took over fifteen years ago, the organization employed 120 people. Today it employs 712, largely developed within the company.

Degussa believes the opportunity for travel and international experience attracts people to it. In order to attain a position in top management, a manager must work a minimum of four years abroad. This view is discussed up-front with potential candidates and is enforced.

The executive committee discusses the list of top employees and assesses them in open discussion. The committee also ranks people within and across functions. They are believers in the ranking process and the discussion that it produces. All of the committee members are very involved in the business; they travel, collect data constantly, and know the management population. They assess people on their total contribution. They do not want just a superior engineer (although they have places for superior engineers); they want a good total contributor and are particularly interested in social competence (defined as being able to go out for a beer after having had a good fight in the business meeting). The ranking discussion flushes these people out as well as establishes the criteria for judging. These rankings are the basis for assessments, bonuses, and promotions.

Salaries are set by following the union negotiations. There is usually a 3 percent annual salary increase. The salary pool is divided up by the executive committee members in discussion with the HR people. There is profit sharing from the division in addition to individual salary and bonus awards.

The division leader will fire or remove to a new position people who are constantly at the bottom of the rankings, along with those who are not contributors and do not fit the company culture. Those who contribute and fit are those who like open communications and live the TQM values.

Leadership

The division leader and the executive committee members are active and visible within the division. Their purpose is to demonstrate TQM values. In addition to the executive committee meetings, they hold "information days" once or twice a year when they visit each plant and R&D site and meet with all employees. The purpose is to spend an equal amount of time explaining what is happening in the business and listening to the views and questions of the people. Every quarter, the committee presents all financial figures to everyone at the sites. They want to create an open system where all information is visible.

The executive committee itself is very active and tries to live the company values. Issues around customers, regions, and functions are discussed in the committee, which meets once a month for about twelve hours in meetings described as being heated. Conflicts are surfaced and debated. Management describes itself as having adopted the values of TQM and being committed to living them. Their goal is to quickly recognize issues that cannot be resolved in customer teams, product teams, and project teams and to resolve them. They describe a decision by the head of manufacturing that was reversed by the manufacturing member of a customer team. The head of manufacturing said the division would not meet a customer request because it could not be done. The team member, probably influenced by the customer business team, said the request would be difficult but that it was easier for Degussa to handle the issue than it was to hand it back to the customer. The team member had a prior and in-depth knowledge of the situation that was superior to that of the manufacturing head.

Degussa's leaders are active in the organization design process and the human resource processes and in resolving conflicts and setting priorities. By living the TQM values and by promoting and rewarding others who behave similarly, they believe they are building a culture that reduces barriers across organizational units and hierarchical levels.

Learnings and Salient Features

Following are the main points from the Degussa case:

- When leaders believe that the organization can be a source of competitive advantage, they design organizations that are exactly that—an organization that is hard to match. Degussa's leaders see their task as designing and improving the organization, choosing and rewarding people who contribute to that organization, and creating the values to sustain the organization's operation.
- Although the formal structure is functional and regional, the organization operates around customers using customer teams, customer business plans, and customer-based performance measures.
- Speed of decision-making results from a combination of a flat structure and an active and effective executive team. There is one level between the customer teams and the executive team. That the leadership at Degussa can quickly address and resolve priority disputes and conflicts is an essential ingredient. The combination of flat structure and active executive team results in decisions that are made at a speed that matches the speed of the business.
- The policies of rotational assignments, participation in a variety of teams, and frequent off-site meetings result in extensive personal networks. The leadership has a policy of valuing these networks and the networkers. The policy results in a situation where all possible organizational dimensions are latent in the network. They can

organize by region, function, customer, product, process, and project. In short, Degussa can organize any way it chooses by creating teams with oversight by the executive committee.

• Organizing around the customer and getting close to that customer allows it to know more about its customers' issues than the customers themselves and competitors do. Degussa, in fact, is smarter about engine catalyst issues than its auto OEM customers are.

• There is room for improvement in Degussa's use of information technology. It admits a deficiency and is working to eliminate it.

4

Medium-Level Application

In this chapter you will learn:

- How to apply the strategy locator to a more complex customer strategy.
- That more complex strategies require more complex organizations.
- How to evolve the organization by building capabilities and then moving to more complex forms.
- How to use customer account units to customize packages for different customers.
- How to use CRM systems in a customer-centric organization.

When a company begins to offer more complex solutions, it requires a more complex organization. In this chapter, the story of an investment bank called IBank is examined. Some five years ago, IBank offered equities, trades, and initial public offerings (IPOs) to its clients. Today it offers equities, convertible bonds, equity derivatives, other IBank products through cross-sell opportunities, and an increasingly diverse set of services. These new services are customized according to the needs of the best customers. In terms of the strategy locator, IBank measured 2 at the beginning of this case. It moved to 3 during the case as the customer-centric unit discovered new customer needs and matched them with new services. IBank used its common brand and customer interactions to customize products and services. But these products and services were mostly stand-alone types, so IBank would measure 2 on the integration scale. It would move from a total score of 4 to 5 during the case and eventually end up with 6. Its position is shown in Figure 4.1.

The organization has evolved in a similar manner. IBank was product-centric and added a light customer-centric unit. This global account management unit of a dozen people is an example of the network integrator role described in Chapter Two. These integrators worked through extensive informal and e-coordination networks using a customer relationship management system. These lateral forms were appropriate for a medium level of solutions integration.

The case described here focuses on the equities business of a global investment bank. The business provides trading in existing equities as its main product. It also provides initial public offerings (IPOs) of new stocks, convertible bonds (which trade like equities), and, more recently, equity derivatives. These products go to a customer who is a fund manager at an institutional investor like Fidelity or Vanguard Group. The customer typically uses the bank's

Figure 4.1 IBank as a Medium Solution Strategy

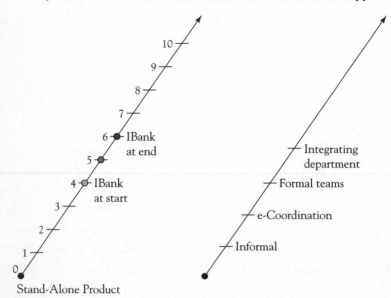

equity trading but may buy one or two other products from the equities business. It may also be possible to cross-sell some products from the treasury products business, like currency derivatives.

The new strategy adopted by the business was to focus on the top fifty accounts and build stronger and closer relationships with them. Then, on the basis of frequent interactions with these customers, the bank would customize services for these top clients. The bank typically offers between two and four products and two to three customized services to a top-fifty customer. These offerings are customized to work together on occasion but are still largely stand-alone products. It also offers some packages of products like a hedge fund starter kit. The bank measures 2 to 3 on both the scale and scope and the integration checklists, giving it a score of 4 to 5.

In contrast to Nestlé or Degussa, the bank is pursuing a more intense customer relationship strategy. Nestlé has chosen thus far to remain product-centric at the corporate level. (It may be more customer-centric within a specific country but not across country subsidiaries.) Recall that Nestlé's approach to customer-focused organization is to use informal networks and e-coordination across countries, and Degussa's is to use formal teams for customers. The bank, as we will see, uses these same lateral coordination mechanisms, but more formally and more intensively. In addition, it has added a small network integrator unit that guides the informal and electronic coordination activities. As is often the case, the bank started at a low level, moved to a medium level, and then, based on experience, is now moving to a higher level of solutions strategy and customer-centricity.

The Global Investment Bank Case

The Global Investment Bank (referred to here as IBank) is part of a worldwide financial services firm. The other two parts of the firm are the Global Consumer Finance and Global Asset Management Groups. IBank and its Global Equities Business are the focus of this chapter. The structure of the investment banking part of the firm is shown in Figure 4.2.

Figure 4.2 IBank Organization Chart

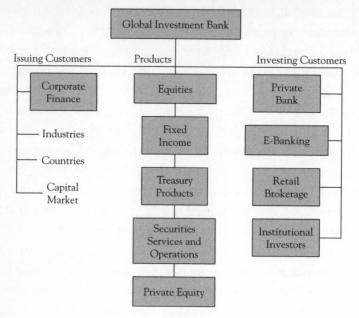

Corporate finance is the customer relationship group responsible for corporate and government issuers of securities. It also contains advisory, underwriting, and mergers and acquisitions activities. There are three product units: for equities, fixed income (bonds), and treasury products (derivatives). Each product consists of a research, sales, and trading unit. There is a private equity business and securities services business, which also is responsible for the operation and trade settlement processing. The securities services is mainly a custody operation where mutual funds must place their stocks and bonds for safekeeping.

The private equity business participates in buyouts and takes equity positions in the companies. The other customers, the investing customers, are shown on the right side of the chart. Private Bank is the private bank for high-net-worth individuals. These people increasingly want access to derivatives and private equity opportunities, so the unit has been made part of the investment bank. A similar argument pertains to e-banking and retail broker-age. Both serve the affluent investor—one over the Internet and the other through a traditional brokerage.

The next sections focus initially on the equities product line and then expand to include the other businesses and their interrelationships.

The Equities Business

A few years ago, the equities product line was a straightforward in-stitutional brokerage business selling equities (primary or IPOs, and secondary) to institutional investors. Each country was a different product. In France, IBank sold French equities to French investors. The transactions were conducted in French francs at the Paris Bourse. The sales calls and trades took place in French. There was some cross-border investing, but the business was similar in Ger-many, Italy, Japan, and elsewhere.

The organization for the equities business was a nearly symmet-rical matrix and is shown in Figure 4.3. In each major country, there were three functions of research, sales, and trading. For the most part, they researched, sold, and traded equities in their own coun-tries. Each function reported to its country manager, who often served as head of equities as well, and to its regional European head. Occasionally there would be a big deal like the IPO of British Air-ways as part of a country's privatization program. In this case, cross-border distribution was an asset.

The selling of equities to fund managers in a country was rela-tively straightforward. The communications followed the simple pattern shown in Figure 4.4.

The research department would generate fifty to one hundred ideas for fund managers to act on. The account manager would pick three to five that were appropriate for the particular fund and fund manager. When a recommendation was accepted, the ac-count manager would instruct trading to execute the buy or sell re-quest. So the fund manager "paid" IBank by executing trades through the bank. IBank made its money on the commission for

Figure 4.3 Equities Organization

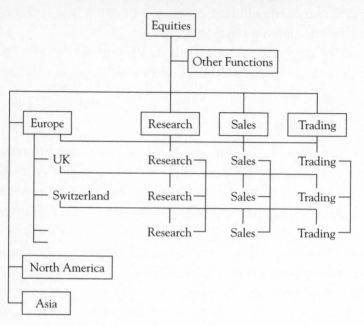

executing trades. The better the fund manager liked the research, the more trades that were executed by IBank. Advantage was obtained through having good IPOs, good relationships, and access to information. In most countries, insider trading was not illegal. Indeed, having networks to get access to insider information was an advantage. The client paid for this information by channeling trades through the equities units' trading function, from which it derived commissions.

The account manager was a generalist who "owned" the client and the revenue stream and was compensated on revenue generated from the client trades. The only person with client contact was the owner of the revenue stream, the account manager. Today just about all of the conditions underlying this traditional model have changed.

Figure 4.4 Traditional Communication Flow

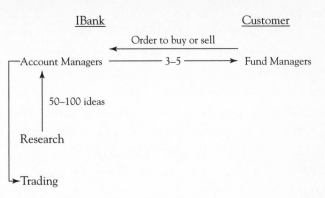

The New Equities Business

In the past decade, almost all of the conditions affecting competition in the equities business have changed and are still changing. Not the least is the widespread availability of financial information to brokers and investors alike, so access to information is disappearing as a competitive advantage, as is insider trading. Instead, new products, new markets, relationships as before, and customized services appear as the sources of advantage going forward. Many of these new offerings are cross-border, cross-product, or cross-functional in nature. The new opportunities create a challenge for the straightforward matrix organization shown in Figure 4.3. They are as follows:

• *Convertible bonds.* Some bonds can be issued at a lower rate if they are convertible into equity at a later date. This financial instrument can be issued for leveraged buyouts and for mezzanine financing of venture investment. After they are issued, the convertibles trade as if they were equities but are still related to bonds.

• *Equity derivatives.* Originally derivatives were cash derivates for hedging changes in interest rates and exchange rates. Today with volatile markets, investors as well as issuers of IPOs and companies engaging in mergers and acquisitions are interested in buying and trading equity derivatives in order to manage their risks during the transition period.

- *Global investment product.* There has been a general adoption of portfolio theory. As markets consolidate and globalize, it is now possible to create portfolios with higher risk-adjusted rates of return. Fund managers are responding to more open markets and cross-border investors by creating global funds. The global fund product is the advice on how to invest $10 billion without any country or sector bias to achieve the best risk-adjusted rate of return.

- *The rise of sectors.* With increased globalization, investors are more interested in investing ideas about telecom or semiconductors than they are about countries. The investment houses are now creating sector funds and are seeking sector investing ideas.

- *The rise of the hedge funds.* As the fund industry consolidates, many of the top fund managers leave and form their own funds, usually a hedge fund. These small funds are one of the most rapidly growing portions of the fund management business. These clients have different needs from mutual funds. For example, they may want to borrow against equities that they own. Now some of the traditional asset management houses are creating their own hedge funds. The service to these customers is to provide loans, short sales, custody, and simultaneous buy and sell transactions.

- *Portfolio trading solution.* Another package of products and services is portfolio trading. This solution is required when a fund wants to restructure its portfolio. For example, the Magellan Fund fired its manager who made a bet on long-term bonds that did not work out. A new manager with a different philosophy came in and restructured the portfolio. This transition is a project, which requires large trades to be executed quickly and discreetly.

A restructuring is a partnership project with the customer. It means working with them on ideas and then executing them. IBank is in a good position in this business because of its trading presence around the world. Trades can be executed in the United States, United Kingdom, Switzerland, Singapore, Australia, and Hong Kong. IBank is one of the three global banks that offer this solution.

• *Using the Internet to distribute research.* Currently, fifty-two hundred clients are on a distribution list, and IBank sends the research as a printed copy and e-mail alerts. IBank believes that this content can be delivered more effectively electronically. It has put its research on the Web site and is making it more user friendly.

• *Leveraging other market segments.* In order to serve existing clients, IBank must invest in new information technology and make itself available on the Internet. It thinks that this enormous investment and increase in capacity can be leveraged across other market segments in addition to the institutional client. In fact, it can leverage its research, products, trading platforms, and settlement systems across these new markets. It can get significant volumes of business by leveraging its scale and geographical presence. IBank believes it can serve as the backroom for small banks, brokerages, private banks, and other intermediaries.

• *Foreign stocks.* The interest in cross-border investing creates an opportunity to sell stocks from other countries to domestic investors. So in large countries, it is possible to sell U.K., Japanese, U.S., German, and French stocks to local investors who are interested in diversification.

• *Special services to large institutional investors.* The investment funds have been consolidating and entering new markets outside their home countries. These large global institutions have a unique set of needs that a large global investment bank can serve.

• *Internet banking.* Using the Internet, IBank could reach affluent investors in countries where it does not have a retail brokerage network and whose citizens are becoming equity investors.

IBank has responded to every one of these opportunities. It has hired and developed specialists in each of these new product and market areas. The lead specialist in each area, usually in the New York or London office, serves as the global product manager for the area. These product managers become the champion for their product or market and hire and train sales specialists for countries with sufficient volume to support specialists. They all report to the global head of sales and distribution. The resulting organization is shown in Figure 4.5.

The structure is the traditional functional-geographical matrix with the champions of the new opportunities as product manager add-ons. In each country, there are the traditional salespeople and account managers for the large customers. Then there is the explosion in the number of sales specialists for all of the new opportunities. All of the specialists want to call on the client fund managers. As a result, the old model of customer interaction cannot work. The account manager is now a bottleneck. But how does the account manager get a complete picture of the account and also customize the services for the client?

Global Account Management

IBank, in response to the changes in the equities business and at the institutional client, created a global account management department and global account directors for its largest customers. The global account directors were to establish and manage top-to-bottom relationships with the large global institutional investors. They were to manage the complex interaction between the IBank specialists and the funds' specialists. On the basis of these interactions, the global account directors were to customize the bank's products and services for clients. Global account management was to serve as the champion for the global account directors and build a CRM system to support the new roles.

Global Account Directors

In 1998, IBank created global account directors for its top fifty clients. Although it had over five thousand clients, 35 percent of its revenue came from the top fifty clients, and this percentage was growing. It decided to create a group of executives whose sole task was to focus on the special needs of these increasingly global players and serve them wherever they are present. Initially, eighteen

Figure 4.5 Organizational Structure of the New Equities Business

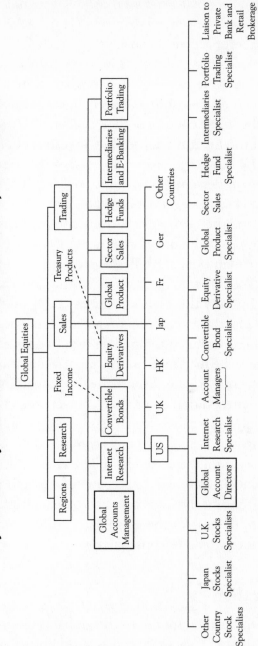

global account directors were selected, and each was given three to four clients. The global account directors were not to be salespeople. They were to be general managers for the account. They were to be managers of account managers.

The global account directors were typically account managers with ten to fifteen years of experience. Many were selected because they had been relationship managers in corporate finance. They resided in the home country of their accounts. They would call on the CEO of the institution, the chief investment officer, the chief strategist, the head of equities, the head of operations, and so on. They were to understand the institution, learn how the institution wanted to do business, get out ahead by knowing the client's long-term plans, and then customize services and products for the client.

The global account directors' other task was to coordinate all of the account managers and salespeople who were calling on the client. One coordination mechanism was the global account plan for the client. Initially this plan was the assembly of all the local account plans plus the global account director's guess as to the increase that could come from customized services. The global account directors were to be measured on this improvement in account revenue and revenue growth. Eventually they began influencing local plans as well. In addition to informal contacts and visits, they held a monthly conference call in which all salespeople and account managers participated. E-mail exchanges completed the communication among the account team members. The relationship between the global account directors and the account team members was informal. The global account directors could participate in the performance management process for these people, but there was no guarantee that their views would be considered.

Customization

The initial internal response to the global account directors was one of skepticism. They were seen as an additional layer and an increase in overhead. But then the situation improved. The global account directors' overall view of the client led them to discover and capitalize on customization opportunities. Eventually these discoveries led to the increase in IBank's ranking at the large clients. The institutional clients allocated their trades and commissions on the basis of their ranking of investment banks. It was the global account director's task to determine what was important to these clients and then get the rest of IBank's departments to respond to the clients' priorities. The clients varied considerably in what they considered to be important. Some clients are interested only in the research from IBank's analysts. One client's fund managers meet every Thursday to discuss a sector like pharmaceuticals. So the global account director, working with the head of research, has the research sectors deliver their latest thinking to this client every Wednesday. Another client does its own proprietary research but values IBank's research database. The global account director, the head of information technology, and the head of research make these data available to the client over the Web and in a format that can be downloaded into the spreadsheets of the client's analysts.

The global account director usually has to work with other departments at IBank, like the research unit, in order to customize services for the client. These directors use their personal networks built up over their ten to fifteen years of experience and their knowledge of the customer to influence others. Their knowledge of the customer is used to increase IBank's ranking and therefore revenues. For example, a number of clients now value flawless execution of trades by operations and include operations quality in their rankings. The global account director and the head of operations try to respond to the clients' needs. In one case, operations created a customer team to synchronize its activities with those of the customer's operations. The leaders of the other departments are also interested in increasing IBank's rankings of these top clients.

Some funds believe that they can get an advantage through aggressive trading. They will call IBank's traders with a "take it or leave it" offer to sell the customer 100,000 shares of IBM at 110 per share. Initially, IBank's traders were reluctant to sell on these terms because they would then have to buy 100,000 shares that might be trading at 111. Working with the head of trading, the global account director worked out some guidelines for dealing with this client. A sales trader was assigned to always take this client's calls. The client's rankings of investment banks' equities division was based 50 percent on their traders' votes of how easy it was to do business with the bank's trading unit. As a result, IBank improved its ranking and revenue from this client.

Some fund managers value face-to-face discussions with the CEO and CFO of the companies whose stock they are buying. In these cases, the global account directors work with relationship managers in corporate finance to schedule these discussions. So the global account directors are primarily charged with knowing the clients, knowing what is important to them, knowing how they vote and rank, and then delivering IBank's resources to serve the client in the manner that the client desires.

Providing Product Line Consulting

Another key activity of the global account director is to obtain access to the client for the product specialists. This access is particularly important for new products. In addition, the global account director's customer knowledge is useful in the creation of new products and cross-selling existing products.

New products create an opportunity to instruct clients and gain access for the product specialist. For example, many funds are eager to start their own hedge funds and use equity derivatives, but they know little about them. On learning of the client's interest, the global account director schedules a conversation between IBank's product specialist and those interested at the client. When the client becomes interested in equity derivatives, the global account director may create a training program for all of the client's fund managers and analysts. The global account director may bring in IBank's training people who have trained all of IBank's people in equity derivatives.

The global fund product provides the same opportunity as equity derivatives and the additional opportunity for a cross-sell. If the client creates a global fund, IBank may then sell its global fund advice to the new global fund manager. The client may choose whether to buy foreign equities for the fund in the United States from the Japan desk, the U.K. desk, or somewhere else. Or it may choose to buy them from IBank Japan and IBank U.K. and then have the shares held by IBank Japan's custody business. Part of the global funds advice may involve treasury products for managing the dollar-yen exchange rate risk. It is the global account director's task to sense the cross-sell opportunity, bring in all of the specialists, support them, and train the client's people to use the new product.

The global account directors can also discover the opportunity for new products. They saw an opportunity to use IBank's global presence as an advantage. As their clients entered in new countries in which IBank was already present, IBank could serve as a host and make it easy for the client to enter these new areas. One of the big investments for the client was starting up its operations and settlement activities in the new country. The global account directors saw the opportunity for a fund to start up quickly and avoid a big investment by outsourcing the client's backroom to IBank's local custody division. The custody division was moving into outsourcing anyway. By working with the global account directors, the custody division developed a starter kit to quickly get the client up and running, with custody handling their outsourced operations. There were numerous opportunities for the global account directors to create value for customers and for the product lines by making links between them on new products and on cross-selling.

Customer Interaction

Managing the interactions with the customer is complex because of the increase in the number of sales specialists at IBank. The interactions are complicated by the increase in the number of specialists at the client. As clients have grown and globalized, they have acquired their own research analysts and traders. The new communications flows are shown in Figure 4.6. The bulk of the conversations now take place between the research analysts. The clients have about 10 percent of the total analysts that IBank has. The fund manager gets advice from the fund's analysts and from the sales, sector sales, various sales specialists, and account managers at the investment banks. When buying or selling, the fund manager instructs the fund's traders who work with the traders and sales traders at IBank. The fund manager then solicits the input of all of these specialists at the client when doing the ranking of the investment banks. This ranking then determines the number of trades executed through IBank.

In addition to the normal informal contacts between global account directors, account managers, and the specialist, IBank has employed a CRM system in order to get a total view of the interactions with clients and to focus them on the issues that the clients think are important. The development and management of the system is the task of the global account management department. Ini-

Figure 4.6   The New Customer Interaction Model

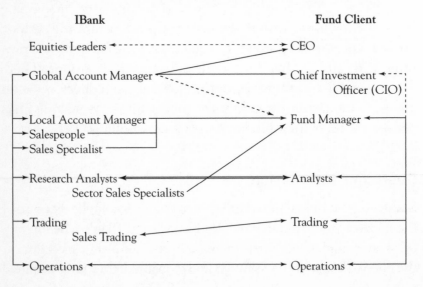

tially each country tracked its own products and clients. The global account management started by focusing on the top fifty clients that were cross-product and cross-border. The CRM tracks all sales and other information about these clients. Each client and its priority are identified. The business plan and goals for the client are posted along with key individuals at the client. The CRM lists all transactions executed for the client, research reports received, and any deals in progress.

A key subsystem of the CRM is the contact management system. Its intent is to be the holy grail of all CRM systems: to record all transactions and conversations with the client. The names of all people at the client with whom IBank does business are listed along with their telephone numbers and e-mail addresses. All people at IBank who contact the client are listed. The contact management system is to be a tool of the global account directors and account managers for getting a total view of what has been said to the client during a day. At every investment bank, the day starts with the morning meeting. The company literally gathers on the sales and trading floors and listens to the head of research, who runs the meeting. At the meeting, research gives its opinion of what is happening, what stocks to recommend, what sectors are hot, what economic news is coming out that day, and what the bank's position is on various issues. The meeting lasts half an hour and ends when trading begins. The IBank people then begin calling their counterparts at clients.

One of the objectives of the contact management system and the global account directors is to coordinate everyone on a daily basis around the morning meeting objectives. First, the content of the morning meeting is posted on the system for all to see what is being recommended to clients this day. There are "talking notes" for discussions with clients. Then an electronic ticker runs along the bottom of the screen throughout the day tracking the current prices of all stocks mentioned in the morning meeting. There are links to research reports for these same stocks and convenient charts like the last twelve months' price history. The salespeople use the data straight off the screen. There is a list of clients whom they are to call, and they are to record whether they spoke to them, left voice mail, or other disposition. There is a chat window, which is intended to record client reactions to the recommendations and to serve as a running commentary throughout the day. The intent is to record people's observations and results of conversations with the clients. There is a cross-sell reward that goes to those who discover opportunities that can be followed up in other departments. Ultimately all conversations from across IBank with a client can be recorded and accessed. In this way, the global account director or account manager can get a complete view of the evolving situation with the client and take whatever actions may be needed.

The contact management system has extensive links with other systems at IBank. One is deal flow, which is maintained by corporate finance. It shows the progress of deals in the pipeline that a client may want to know about. Event management lists all upcoming events in which the client may be interested. Prior to the issuance of a big offering, the issuing company's management may appear at an event for possible buyers. Or IBank may hold an annual e-commerce event. A third link is to the Web site, which is electronically accessible to clients. One site is Investment Banking On-Line (IBOL). All the top fifty have a customized home page. It is the portal for all areas of the bank. Like the global account director, IBOL is to deliver the firm to the client. Most clients, however, go directly to product Web sites on a daily basis. Fixed Web is the fixed income site and increasingly allows more direct or on-line trading. The equity site allows on-line trading for a few large clients. The trend is for more on-line trading. The global account director or account manager can complete the picture of client activity with a scan of the e-access sites.

Global account management is working to realize the intent of the system—a single integrated interface with which to interact with the client. Initially the system was too complex, so it is being simplified. It was also to serve the company and, less often, to serve the needs of the people who were expected to provide information.

So global account management is trying to find ways to deliver benefits to users as well as asking them for input. The experienced salespeople still feel that they own the customer relationship and are reluctant to open the relationship to everyone. The official position, however, is that the client is an IBank client, and new salespeople are adapting to this position. Global account management has also contributed to the design of a reward system that considers people's behavior when using the contact management system.

The equities group has developed its own peer ranking system to determine compensation. This system, in its second year, was created by an internal working group to reward all the contributions people made over and above meeting their numbers. With so many specialists having to work together around clients and products, the equities group runs on cooperative efforts. In this system, everyone in equities ranks all of the people they work with in all of the departments. There are four categories with descriptions attached. The system is Web based and easy to use. The results are gathered by the leadership and used to rank people in quartiles. These rankings become the basis of individual bonuses.

Global account management is also training all internal people in these systems. One session is devoted to client relationship management. Another is to teach the contact management system to the same people. In addition, the sessions are an important source of feedback on how well the initiatives are working and of new ideas for improvement. For the contact management system, the leadership of the unit being trained follows up to monitor use. Unless everyone uses it, the system becomes less valuable. Currently global account management is searching for ideas and debating whether to use carrots or sticks or a mixture to encourage universal use. One approach is to put trip expense reimbursement on the system. Travelers do not get reimbursed until they have entered their contact report into the system. The ultimate goal of the initiative is to allow the global account director or account manager to manage the client relationship without being a bottleneck and insisting that all contacts go through him or her. In simpler times, almost all contacts could go through the account manager. Today the proliferation of specialists at the investment bank and the client, combined with the pace of the business, make one point of contact impossible.

These contacts will be replicated in each of three or four large countries. In order to manage the relationship, the global account directors use all the tools that are available. The process starts with a client plan for the year. This plan may involve a gathering of as many contact people as possible to brainstorm and create the plan. These sessions teach people about the top fifty in general and this client in particular. The session provides a face-to-face meeting of as many team members as possible. The plan is then put on the contact management system, and members can get a context within which to conduct their daily contacts. The plans get updated every six months. The global account directors conduct monthly telephone calls with the core members of the client team to exchange information and review progress against plan. And finally there is the constant daily informal contact that takes place between various specialists serving the account.

One of the purposes of the contact management system is to convert this informal contact to a more organized and informed process. The global account directors try to use it all day long. As they walk the floors, they encourage their teams to use it. They show how it can be useful to the users. They show how much knowledge IBank has about the client and how the specialist can use it to better serve customers and increase sales. As more people use the contact management system and as more improvements are added, the global account directors and account managers will improve their ability to present an integrated, customized service for top clients.

Customer Relationships at IBank

The change at IBank is shown in the star model in Figure 4.7. The strategy was to focus on the top fifty customers, build close relationships with them, customize services for these clients, and cross-sell when possible. The structure change was to add a global account management for these top fifty customers. The key processes were customer planning, customer relationship management, and the multiple informal communication networks. A powerful shaper of behavior at all investment banks is the reward system. IBank used rankings of personnel by all people and the global account directors as well. These rankings were to focus all people on the customers and customization for the top fifty. There was extensive training in the contact management system and development and selection of relationship-oriented global account directors. Together these policies have created a medium version of a customer-centric organization that requires midrange levels of both scale and scope and integration of solutions.

Next Steps in Global Account Management

The leaders of IBank made a review of the global account directors at the end of two years. They made several changes in order to strengthen the approach. They are moving from the medium to a higher level of customer-centricity.

Figure 4.7   People and Integration of Solutions

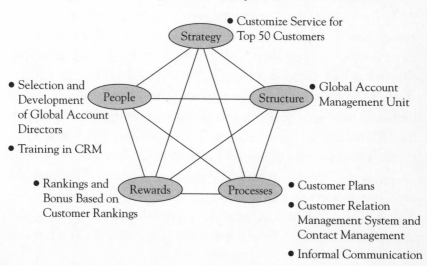

The review showed that the internal acceptance and understanding of client-centric activities at IBank was variable. At first, global account directors were seen as a level of overhead. Then IBank created a course in client relationship management to create a common understanding. The course also became a source of feedback on how well the global account directors were working and a source of ideas for improvement. But even with understanding, there was variable acceptance among country and account managers. Some are naturally cooperative and play the reciprocity game of giving and getting favors. When they are matched with senior global account directors with good networks and networking skills, the system works. However, there are country managers who are interested only in their country revenue and not in diversions that do not enhance that revenue. These managements are already pressed by 20 to 50 percent growth rates in the sale of equities. New, small, demanding foreign funds producing little or no revenue are an annoyance. If these same managers are willing to move from firm to firm, concrete performance numbers are more valuable than firm-specific goodwill from reciprocity. The response at IBank is to select and reward country managers who are skilled at reciprocity and to remove and deny bonuses to those who are not. The collapse of equity markets after 2000 also helped country managers see the global funds as a new source of growth.

The review showed a variety of reactions from customers. Some preferred to do business as they always have, country by country. Other customers were skeptical at first and then through dialogues with the global account directors came to find value. The CIO of a large U.K. fund complained to the global account director that the fund's new Japanese office was not receiving research reports from IBank's Japanese subsidiary. The subsidiary was not sending research because the client had placed no orders with it and did not know that the client had established a presence. The Japanese subsidiary began sending research at the global account director's request. The CIO then asked about equity derivatives. The global account director brought in a specialist to educate the CIO. Eventually all of the client's fund managers went through IBank's two-day course on derivatives. This CIO became a convert. Other clients had similar experiences because IBank was one of the first to offer a global account service. At the other extreme were some clients who refused to do business with an investment bank that did not have a global account director assigned to them. They valued the service and particularly the hosting service when they entered Japan and Hong Kong.

On the basis of the review, IBank further segmented its clients. Segment 1 was the top fifty plus other clients who wanted to do business in the traditional way, country by country and product by product. The account manager in the client's home country acted as the global account director when the role was needed. Segment 2 consisted of clients who wanted to do business product by product but wanted a global account director to coordinate within equities across countries. And finally, in segment 3, there were increasing numbers of clients who wanted the global account director to coordinate across countries and products. IBank then adopted a policy of doing business the way the customer wanted to do business. It also adopted a strategy of migrating clients from segment 1 to segments 2 and 3. IBank was the first and one of the few that could provide global account directors to serve these clients. These changes moved IBank to a 3 on the integration scale as well as the scale and scope. That gave it a 6 total for the strategy.

IBank made several changes to its organization in order to implement the focus on segments 2 and 3. These changes are shown in Figure 4.8.

The segment 2 global account directors were placed in a separate organization within equities to serve the segment 2 clients. The account managers serving segment 2 clients would report to the global account director and the country manager. The planning process would result in the country managers' having goals for local clients and goals for segment 2 and 3 clients. IBank and the global account management department continued their work to develop client profit and loss accounting systems.

Figure 4.8 New Global Account Segment Structure

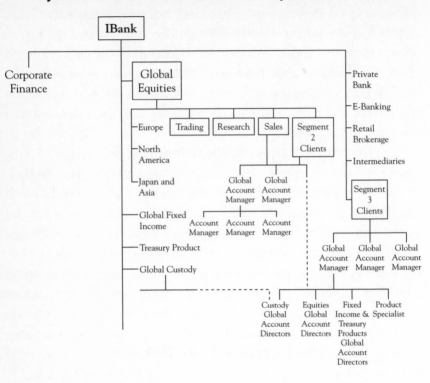

The other change was a creation of a segment 3 client group. This group reported directly to the head of IBank. These clients were assigned a global account manager. These managers had only one client. Reporting to them were the global account directors and account managers serving these clients for all product lines and countries. The accounting and planning systems are crucial for this segment. One client does business with all of IBank's product lines. It pays directly for the custody service. But for the others, it chooses to pay by directing trades through IBank's Treasury Products in the United Kingdom. This payment scheme is most efficient for this customer. It is up to IBank to sort out the revenues and credit the right product lines and countries.

The bonus system has also been changed to reflect the structural changes. The bonus process starts with the determination of the bonus pool based on IBank's total profits. The bank's pool is then subdivided into pools for corporate finance, the product lines, and the customer sets. The pool is divided on profits versus plan and other goals. Some amount is usually held back to reward individuals over and above the bonus awarded through the organizational process. The segment 3 client organization will get a pool to be distributed based on its performance against plan.

The equities division also receives a pool to be divided among its units. Originally the pool was divided among the countries, which then allocated bonuses to sales, trading, and research. Today, the equities unit emphasizes its global nature and divides the pool first among sales, trading, research, and, after the reorganization, segment 2 clients. The global account directors and managers now have a major voice in the bonus allocation. Their voice in the reward system is a major change and a major step toward a more customer-centric orientation.

Lessons from IBank

There are a number of lessons that can be taken from the IBank case:

• Different customers want to do business differently. IBank applied the principle of "Do business the way the customer wants to do business." It learned that not every customer wants a single global interface, although some do. So it customized the relationship. Some clients worked with product sales in the countries. Some worked with the segment 2 organization across borders. And others worked with the segment 3 unit across borders and products.

• Advantage through managing complexity. The price of customizing relationships was a more complex IBank structure. However, the complexity created value for many of the top customers. IBank attained an advantage because many other investment banks could not provide the global coordination service.

• Growth through customization. On the basis of customer interaction, the global account directors were able to deliver customized research, trading, and operations services. They were able to deliver education for new products like equity derivatives. There is no limit to the number of customer needs that can be discovered and served.

- Managing customer interactions. The IBank case provides a good example of managing customer interactions at all touch points. In today's business world, where specialist talks to specialist, the CRM model is needed. IBank created a global account director who is not a salesperson but a manager of the account relationship. Through mechanisms like the account plan, monthly conference calls, walking the floor, and e-mail, the global account director can get an overall picture and influence a common, consistent approach. The contact management electronic system is a major advance. It does not work perfectly yet. But through training, promotion by global account directors and supervisors, improved ease of use, and rewards, it is becoming a useful tool.

- The emergence of customer-centric units. The single approach to the customer through segments 2 and 3 is a step toward the creation of customer-facing organizations. It is a major step toward creating a customer-centric capability and using it to learn about customers, customize offerings for them, and create value through bundling products in useful ways.

- Link the customer units with the product units. Once a separate customer unit is formed, it needs to be linked to the product units. The segment 3 organization shows a global account manager as the leader and global account directors from the product lines. These global account directors are the primary links as they work for both the product and the customer. They participate in creating a customer plan and goals that align the product and customer interests. The necessary product and customer accounting systems, pricing policies, and double-counting revenue are also implemented.

- The IBank case shows the customer interaction and customization that is required by many customers today. It also shows some limited bundling of products into solutions and outsourcing of client activities.

5

Complete-Level Application

In this chapter you will learn:

- How to apply the strategy locator to the most complete solutions strategies.

- How IBM created an organization that can act as "One Company."

- The definition of the front-back organization model, which combines a customer-centric front end with a product-centric back end.

- The difference between horizontal generic solutions and vertical industry-specific solutions.

- How formal processes like CRM are used to manage the complex interfaces that go with high scale and scope solutions.

- How a solutions profit and loss unit spans the entire company.

- About the kinds of human resource practices that are needed to support customer-centric organizations.

Welcome to complexity. While it can be argued that applying the customer-centric capability at this highest level offers the most challenges, it can also be viewed as offering the most—perhaps only—relief to the corporation whose customer relationships will not be expedited by anything less. Further solace may be gleaned in the knowledge that there is more delineation available for the front-back hybrid model—the lateral networking capability requisite for this level of implementation—than for lower lateral network models. The corporation that goes for the big guns finds a deeper degree of support available, not unlike a high-roller who gets keys to the penthouse suite (though gambling parallels should not be inferred).

IBM offers a range of solutions, but many of them will measure 5 on the scale and scope strategy dimension. The use of standards in the computer industry prevents it going all the way on the integration. Thus, a score of 4 on integration gives it a total of 9 on the strategy locator (Figure 5.1).

Complex Solutions and Customer-Centric Organizations

This chapter describes companies that measure high on the scale and scope of the solutions they offer. At the same time, this large number of products and services must work together closely, as with

Figure 5.1 IBM as the High-Complexity Model

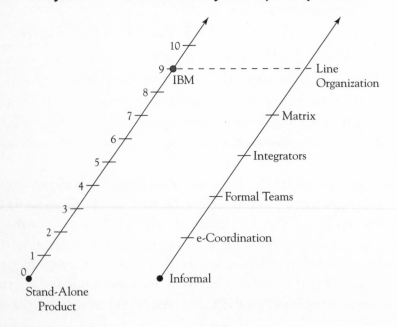

computer systems. When the components of solutions must work together closely, so must the product divisions that design and produce these components. The solutions provider must also know how to put all these products and services together for the customer. Hence, it must have a customer-centric organization that has the in-depth customer knowledge as to how to create solutions that customers value. The product divisions must work together not only among themselves but also with the customer-centric units. Designing these organizations is the focus of this chapter and the next.

In this chapter we study one of the best implementers of the customer-centric capability: IBM. The following chapter analyzes the high-level application of two other companies and discusses the alternatives in implementation used by corporations with structures and requirements different from those of IBM.

IBM

In the early 1990s, IBM was product-centric and focused on hardware products such as mainframes. It shows that a company can successfully add a customer-centric capability and use it to deliver solutions. This chapter provides a detailed look at the steps, the challenges, and the payoffs involved in IBM's successful implementation of the customer-centric capability.

Parts of the IBM success story are well known. Lou Gerstner's decision not to break up IBM because customers wanted all the capabilities kept together is an example. Less well known is the transformation of the organization to get all of the parts of IBM to act together.

IBM, like all of the other computer companies, offers the largest scale and scope solutions. They offer combinations of hardware, software, and service products that are combined into solutions for supply chain management (SCM) or customer relationship management (CRM). And these solutions must function in an integrated manner on a twenty-four-hour, seven-day-a-week basis. The integration needs are lessened somewhat by having products that are modular. That is, the computer business is increasingly characterized by open standards driven by customers who do not want to be dependent on a single supplier of proprietary systems. IBM has embraced these open standards but still has a formidable organization design challenge.

Strategy

The decision to keep IBM together was a key one that shaped the future strategy. On the basis of extensive discussions with customers, Gerstner and IBM's leadership learned that customers did not want to build their own systems in the face of rapidly changing technologies and products that were difficult to integrate. IBM could do the integration and everything else for them. Under one roof, IBM had the hardware, software, and, soon, the services to do the whole task for the customer. It also had the relationships and global presence to serve these customers. The leaders came to realize that IBM's size and scope, thought to be a weakness in the product-centric world, was a source of uniqueness and advantage in providing customer solutions.

In 1995, the leaders announced the "New IBM," which was to be based on network-centric computing and the Five S's (servers, standards, services, software, and solutions). Networks of computers were seen to tie together all of a customer's activities, usually using software like SAP's enterprise resource planning (ERP) system. The twenty-first-century networks were seen to be a corporation's lifeblood and principal means of commerce. IBM invested in Lotus Notes and other groupware packages to reinforce the new network concept. It also financed a redesign of the hardware line to support communications as well as computing.

Another important decision was to orient all of IBM to the Internet. Initially the Internet was part of the network-centric computing strategy. IBM also had its own private network. It was not clear in 1995 whether private networks or the Internet would dominate, but once it became clear to IBM, it focused on the Internet;

it sold its private network to AT&T and got out of Prodigy, its proprietary network service. About a year ahead of Microsoft, IBM shifted focus. It also gets high marks for not focusing on the browser war, although it had one of its own. From the beginning, IBM and Gerstner have seen the Internet as a means of conducting business transactions.

The move to the Internet was to be led by the newly created Internet Division, part of the Software Group. The Internet represents the "New IBM." It was network computing based on ease of use and open standards to which IBM was now committed. The Internet Division initially worked with all of the product divisions to make sure that its products were Internet ready. The division then put together IBM's Internet strategy and a list of products and offerings that an Internet-ready IBM needed but lacked at that time. In 1996, IBM announced its e-business strategy. The purpose was to show customers how they could transform themselves into Internet-based companies. Not surprisingly, this e-commerce strategy plays to IBM's strengths. When a company makes its Web site its front door, that door is open twenty-four hours a day and seven days a week. When all transactions take place on the network in a 24-7 world, that becomes IBM's world. The customer needs 100 percent available servers, huge storage capability, secure databases, massive processing power, expert systems integration, consulting help, training, financing, security advice, and services to pull it all together. Pulling it together as customer solutions is the New IBM. But the thrust of the Internet strategy is also to accentuate software and services. With hardware prices and margins falling, IBM had long been seen as vulnerable. The Internet was its way out of dependence on hardware.

Gerstner stated his view of services in IBM's 1998 Annual Report: "The greatest competitive advantage in the information technology industry is no longer technology. . . . Technology changes much too quickly now for any company to build a sustainable competitive advantage on that basis alone. Someone is always inventing some software code or device that is a little faster or cheaper.

More and more, the winning edge comes from *how you help customers use technology*—to steal a march on their competitors to implement entirely new business models. That means creating integrated solutions that draw on the full range of products and increasingly, services" (p. 6).

The real payoff of services is believed to be in solutions packages of hardware, software, and services. At IBM, these are created by the industry groups when they are industry specific, or vertical (for example, computer-aided design for manufacturing companies), or by global services when they are applicable across industries, or horizontal.

An example of vertical solutions comes from the global insurance solutions practice, which generates $5 billion in revenue each year from two thousand accounts. The practice has developed a strategy to be a catalyst in the industry and to take the first steps in creating enterprise architectures. These architectures will allow insurance companies to migrate from legacy systems to the Internet. A key ingredient in the strategy is the Insurance Research Center (IRC), which was created as part of IBM's research laboratories. The IRC also works through a "live engagement lab," the Insurance Solution Development Center (ISDC) in La Hulpe, Belgium. There, researchers work with lead customers on developing applications. Through the IRC and ISDC, the practice is working to create a portfolio of solutions (called offerings) for the future based on enterprise architectures, the Internet, data mining, and voice, data, and video technologies.

IBM's answer for infrastructure is the insurance application architecture (IAA), which was designed with forty insurance and financial services companies. It is intended to define common components and services that can be applied across all insurance lines and thereby lower the costs and risks connected with creating new systems. IBM plans to tailor IAA through packaged insurance business systems to meet the requirements of different customers. Within this new architecture, the insurance practice has launched three initiatives for its customers.

First-of-a-kind solutions are joint research projects with customers—for example:

- Collaborative Internet sales and marketing, a prototype that enables customers, agents, and representatives to simultaneously view a screen and talk to each other using voice, data, and video
- Underwriting profitability analysis, a data mining technology used on existing customer and policy data
- Hand-held terminals, that is, the use of mobile devices that communicate with and deliver customer and policy data to insurance company sales forces

InsureCommerce is an offering consisting of a family of solutions to bring companies into e-commerce using Java software. It consists of several solutions:

- InsureStrategy, consulting and services for developing an Internet strategy
- InsureIntra, an intranet and Internet design and implementation service combined with legacy system integration
- InsureKiosk, which enables insurance providers to extend their marketing and services by deploying kiosks in strategically placed locations
- InsureAgent, an agent automation and data-sharing product to manage agents more effectively

Third is the transformation of key processes in insurance operations such as claims management. IBM is integrating agency management and information systems with CRM solutions to create consistent construction of databases. The CRM solution also integrates with call centers. IBM is also targeting lines of business in insurance with solutions for life, health, and property and casualty.

All of these insurance solutions are combinations, to various degrees, of IBM hardware, software, and services and partners' hardware, software, and services. In each case, IBM integrates the components into a solution or offering for the customer. The offerings combine all of IBM in the service of the insurance customer.

The same types of solutions are developed by global services when the solution is not industry specific and can be leveraged across industries and applications. Indeed, the e-Business Services unit sees itself creating repeatable solutions. Among these offerings are supply chain management, e-commerce, customer relationship management, and ERP. For each of these, there is a global offering owner who coordinates the development, improvement, and deployment of the solutions. These solutions can be built by IBM and turned over to the customer to run, they can be built and outsourced to IBM to run for the customer, or the application could be hosted on IBM's computers and sold by means of a service fee.

One of these offerings is Business Intelligence (BI), which was launched in February 1998. It is a combination of hardware (servers, storage), software (its database product DB2, data mining), and services (consulting, education, installation, maintenance) for data mining and data warehousing for large customer databases. It can be combined into CRM systems as well. The offering was a companywide initiative to address a $70 billion per year opportunity. There are twenty-five hundred specialists in the field today selling and implementing these systems, along with a partnership program of 150 vendors. The applications are designed to help companies make more informed decisions about markets, risk assessments, and classification of customers into segments and to manage marketing campaigns. An early adopter was Citibank's Consumer Banking unit. Citi is using a portfolio of services to help quantify the lifetime value of its customers. Empire Blue Cross is using it along with IBM software called Fraud and Abuse Management System to uncover medical fraud. It led to $4 million in savings in 2000.

The network-centric computing strategy was implemented through the Five S's: servers, standards, software, services, and solutions. Today, network-centric computing has been transformed into "Business on Demand" by the new CEO, Sam Palmisano. Business on Demand is the movement of computing to servers run by service providers like IBM, with applications delivered as a service from the Internet. Solutions are still a central part of the offering to customers. So if solutions were a reason for keeping IBM together, how did the leadership get it to act together?

IBM Structure

The IBM structure before Gerstner arrived always had a strong geographical orientation. It was based on IBM Americas and the World Trade Corporation, which served the rest of the world. The key positions outside the United States were the country managers. After losing some outsourcing contracts because some country managers opted out of bidding, the structure was changed to the front-back model shown in Figure 5.2.

IBM's structure is constantly changing, as are a number of the service-offering titles. The structure shown here is simplified, but captures the essence of it and uses more generic titles like *outsourcing*. It shows the four-dimensional design of most high-level customer-centric companies. Reporting to the CEO or office of the chief executive are the functions. These are corporate staff units, most of whose members are working in the product lines and industry groups. The back end of the structure consists of product lines for hardware, software, and services. They design, deliver, and sell their products to IBM customers. Global services also has a product management type of responsibility in addition to selling and delivering services. This product management activity is to create horizontal solutions ("offerings" in IBM language) that are not industry specific. For example if a customer wants to implement a CRM project, IBM would want to provide the initial consulting, change management, systems integration, education, and then either the supporting hardware and software or the outsourcing of the service. The product manager, known as an offering owner, would coordinate the various

Figure 5.2 IBM Structure

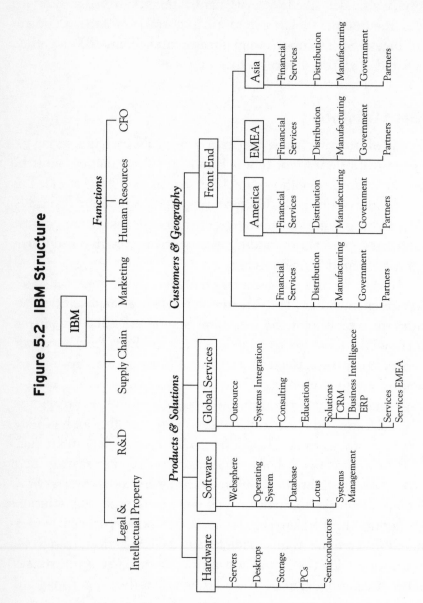

businesses to create several different types of CRM offerings. So both the global services and software groups have charters to deliver all of IBM to the customer for offerings and initiatives.

The front end of the structure is based on customers collected into industry groups (such as financial services customers) and geography. The industry groups focusing on the largest one thousand global customers replaced the countries as the central building block of the sales and distribution structure. In this four-dimensional structure, the product lines are the profit centers. The industry groups are not yet profit centers but instead are measured on revenue and margins. P&Ls are added up for geographies, but they do not function as profit centers.

In order to examine the customer organization in more detail, let us look at the Europe, Middle East, and Africa (EMEA) region. It represents IBM in microcosm but without the manufacturing activities. The structure is shown in Figure 5.3. Reporting to the general manager of EMEA are product lines (hardware sales, software, global services), industries, country operations, and functions (finance and planning, legal, human resources, and marketing). It is the same four-dimensional structure that reports to the CEO. The actual work is done by following processes that connect these four dimensions. The European portion operates primarily through following opportunities and offerings.

Opportunities

One of Gerstner's early moves was to reengineer the business processes at IBM. At one point there were thirteen global processes being redesigned and led by global process owners. Initially these processes were put on the IBM network. Today they are on intranets and extranets. One of the key processes described here is IBM's own CRM.

One of the processes that integrate IBM around the customer is a subsystem of the CRM called the Opportunity Management System (Omsys). An opportunity is originated by salespeople when a

Figure 5.3 IBM Europe, Middle East, and Africa Front-End Structure

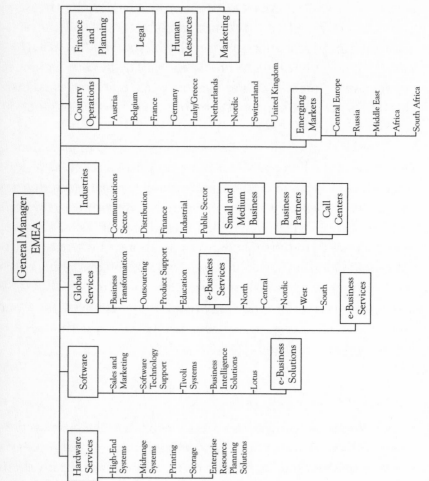

Note: Titles have been modified for this structure.

customer sales opportunity appears (although anyone can originate an opportunity). Some opportunities are product opportunities (for example, a customer orders a replacement mainframe). These orders are straightforward opportunities and are probably handled automatically over the Internet. The challenge is when integration is required, as when a customer like DaimlerChrysler announces the construction of a new assembly plant in Alabama. It would like IBM to bid on supplying the entire package of hardware, software, maintenance, installation, financing, and even outsourcing. For these opportunities, a team from across IBM must swing into action. This type of opportunity is the coordination challenge for delivering IBM to the customer.

Omsys is part of the whole CRM process, which is driven by the industry groups. They begin the process with a customer plan. There is a plan for the largest one thousand customers, like Daimler-Chrysler. The purpose is to get ahead of the process, anticipate events like a new factory, and begin assembling the resources. The plan for each customer is prepared by a customer team with members from around the world. It is to anticipate sales for that customer from anywhere in the world that the customer is present. For the largest and most profitable customers, product specialists assist in preparing their part of the plan as well. Each customer set has product people dedicated to it for preparing its plans. High-end systems salespeople will be dedicated to the banking industry or even to Citigroup when there is enough volume to justify the dedication. These people will report to both their product line and their industry.

These plans accomplish several goals. They lead to a plan for the industry, revenue targets and quotas for the people, and a forecast for the resources needed from the product lines to support the customers. Second, the planning process allows the prioritization of opportunities and of customers. The CRM is based on the value of the customers. Not all customers are equal. The most profitable and desirable customers get the highest priorities. Some opportunities also get a higher priority. Banks in the Nordic region lead the industry in technology. These opportunities will be given a priority to get the industry firsts. Third, the planning process is a means to build the customer team and teach the product specialists about the customer's situation. The account manager in the customer's home country leads the team and the planning effort. The industries put the plans together and set the industry and customer priorities. The top customers are also assigned to the top two hundred executives within IBM. Each executive has two to six customers for whom she or he acts as the executive partner.

The sales link process takes these plans for industries and converts them into expected sales numbers for the product lines. The product lines then prepare to meet these targets and provide the resources. The targets are adjusted quarterly. IBM is in a volatile market where conditions can change quickly. For example, a customer hires a new chief information officer, who shifts the company from Unix to NT. A pharmaceutical customer is surprised and has its revenue reduced when its new drug fails to win approval from the Food and Drug Administration. The customer then postpones its acquisition of new information technology equipment.

Omsys works within this planning context. The system starts when an opportunity is entered from a salesperson, a reseller, or over the Internet. It is immediately evaluated within the system by comparing it to benchmarks and prioritizing it. It is possible not to pursue the opportunity, but usually it is qualified and assigned an opportunity owner. If the opportunity is like the replacement mainframe, the owner will be the product line salesperson from mainframes. If it is the bid opportunity from DaimlerChrysler, the owner will likely be the DaimlerChrysler account manager in Stuttgart. The opportunity will be indicated on the screens of the product representatives on the DaimlerChrysler team. They will gather the resources from their specialty to staff the bid team. These specialists will be selected on the basis of availability of the talent and the priority assigned to DaimlerChrysler and the Alabama opportunity.

Many simple opportunities (add a thousand seats to a Lotus Notes license) pass through the CRM system without human intervention. But there are numerous chances for disagreements on complex and new opportunities. There are the usual differences where a salesperson sees a great revenue opportunity and the product line sees a poor profit opportunity. Then there is always the bottleneck caused by the hot resource. In the past, the scarce resource was SAP programmers, then it was Java programmers, and now there are too few Linux programmers. The opportunity owner then begins an escalation process. She goes to her network first. Does she know anyone who could help get the resources she needs? If not, she can search the skills database. If still not, she can go to her executive partner or the industry head to see if their contacts can help. If still no, there is the senior leadership team, the EMEA head, and direct reports, which meets weekly or the European growth team, a smaller group that meets when needed. During this process, the participants should have been prepared by the planning process. The scarce resource is allocated to the opportunity owner, or not, based on the company priority for that opportunity. Then once an opportunity, like DaimlerChrysler in Alabama, is won, an execution or an engagement team is activated to complete the opportunity. These resources are allocated in the same manner as those for the bid team.

Another issue at all companies providing solutions is the pricing of the offering and dividing of revenue among the various profit centers that contribute to the solution. At IBM, these decisions are made at pricing centers. Some centers are global, others are regional (EMEA), and still others may be local in small and medium businesses (SMBs). The pricing centers are run by finance. They allocate revenues to product lines, hardware, software, and services, based on pricing methodologies that they have developed over the years. They call them "fair share" methods. The system is administered by the network of chief financial officers who support the profit centers. It is legitimate to appeal to this group if a share of a deal is not seen to be fair. The network tries to be fast and fair and tries to follow Gestner's priorities: (1) win the opportunity, (2) optimize for IBM, and (3) optimize for your profit center. The CFO tries to use 360-degree feedback to reinforce the norm.

All opportunities, once entered, are available for tracking. Omsys can answer various questions. How many opportunities do we have at DaimlerChrysler? Who is working on them? And so on. IBM is creating Web sites for its most important customers, a variation on MY.IBM.Com, a personalized customer Web site. In 2002, IBM had two thousand customers with their own sites for direct ordering, customer service, and inquiries. In this manner, the CRM process is the means by which resources from across IBM can be matched and integrated around customer opportunities.

Offerings

The other process for matching and integrating resources is in the creation of offerings. Offerings are solutions that can require hardware, software, and service products from inside and outside IBM that need to be integrated to solve a customer issue. Some of the offerings are industry specific and fall within the industry customer set. The solutions described earlier for the insurance business would be the responsibility of the insurance solutions unit in the finance sector. When the offering cuts across industries, the owner is usually in global services. The e-business offerings tend to be located in global services and specifically in the e-business services unit. In each case, the purpose of the offering is to cannibalize the one-offs and create repeatable solutions. These solutions can be global like e-commerce, ERP, CRM, supply chain, and so on. Some can be regional like the move to the euro and the European Monetary Union. Others can be local like applications for chartered accountants in southern France. For each offering, there is an offering owner who acts as a product manager creating a new product. The owner formulates a strategy, usually with the help of a cross-IBM team. When approved, the strategy implementation is led by the owner, who reports at milestones along the way. The industry, the region, or the company selects those offerings as being worthy of reuse and the effort to standardize them.

An offering is created through the cooperation of many IBM organizations. For example, IBM is working with a manufacturing customer in a business very much like IBM's own business. This project is a full partnership effort to implement CRM and e-commerce, as IBM has implemented them in its own organization. The partnership consists of the industry group, global services, the software group (especially middleware), R&D, and some input from the hardware side. Usually the offerings are created using existing hardware architectures. In another effort, the best people from around the world are working on developing an offering with a European bank. Both offerings have been globally prioritized by the leadership of IBM. Others can be prioritized by the European leadership. So by working with lead, often large, customers, IBM can develop solutions, which can become offerings.

The organization of a global offering unit is shown in Figure 5.4. The majority of the offerings are located in e-business services (see the EMEA organization chart). The one shown here is in the outsourcing business because it is a hosting offering. Specifically, it is the e-business hosting services in which IBM is the host for an application that serves the customer. That is, IBM owns the hardware and software and runs the infrastructure. The customer pays for the service by the number of persons using it, the transaction, or by the month.

There are three subofferings with a product manager in charge of each. One is Web hosting. The customer may create a Web site and control its content, and IBM runs the infrastructure and the application on its own servers. Or IBM can build and run the Web site for the customer. Application services is used when IBM becomes an application services provider. That is, IBM will host the ERP application from SAP or J. D. Edwards, CRM from Siebel, and so on. There are about ten applications currently available, and new ones are being added constantly. Trading networks is where IBM hosts a market for business-to-business transactions. Working with a partner, IBM creates a market like e-chemicals. It will then build and

Figure 5.4   Structure of a Global Solution Offering

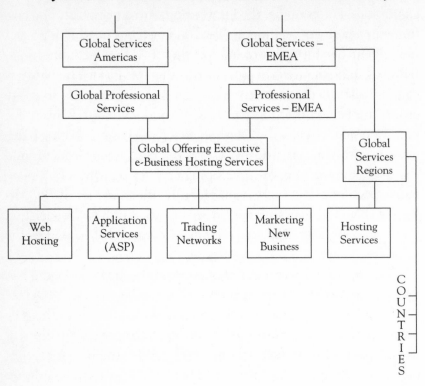

run the infrastructure and sell the service by the transaction. The partner will bring the industry expertise and run the market. Again, new markets are constantly being added. The addition of new markets and applications is the charter of the marketing department.

When a new application is discovered, it is proposed in the business plan. When it is funded, an owner is appointed and a team created to formulate a strategy and form a project to implement the offering. The hosting offering teams work closely with software for Web servers, firewalls, encryption, and other middleware. They work with the server group to deliver the hardware. Usually they use existing hardware, but on one occasion they needed modifications to the servers and operating systems to support the hosting of an e-commerce activity. The global services business took the issue to the IBM technical committee to get a priority for a hardware and software project. The technical committee is the top organizational body in IBM for deciding on new products and technologies. It is run by the head of technology and includes the CEO in its membership. The request was approved, and a product owner was created to lead the project. These projects report every two months to the technical committee until all work is closed out.

The new offerings are then taught to global services salespeople and members of customer account teams, which bid for and implement the opportunities from customers. For hosting services, there are some seven hundred people globally distributed in the field for sales and implementation. These people often work with the industry groups to originate opportunities. Global services has its own sales specialists for its product lines. These sales and implementation people are organized by region and report through the global services organization.

The global head of hosting services is considered to be a "lite P&L." That is, the main P&Ls within global services are the regions and then the products, like outsourcing. An offering is coded when an opportunity arises and is captured. By associating the offering code with the opportunities, a revenue stream can be identified and matched with costs. These opportunities enter the system through Omsys. The offering owner responds when customer interests are flagged as offering opportunities.

Other opportunities are organized similarly but are housed in e-business services. There are five basic offerings: ERP, e-commerce, supply chain management, CRM, and business intelligence. For these offerings, the customer invests in the hardware and software to run them rather than have IBM host them as an applications service provider. In addition to the hardware and software, IBM provides the consulting, change management, systems integration, installation, availability services, and education. Many of these offerings are scalable. A customer can begin in e-commerce with a home page hosted by IBM. A medium-sized business can begin with "Start Now." Similarly a customer can begin with ERP I and move to ERP II and III. These offerings and offering structures are common across all of the regions of IBM and the regions within global services EMEA.

So much of the integration of IBM product lines and industries takes place through processes to create and implement offerings and to capture and deliver opportunities. The CRM process with its subprocesses for Omsys and SalesLink provides a common means for coordination. But the analysis needs to go a step further. In organizing around the customer, IBM has created customer sets like the industries. But every product line, service, and offering has its own sales force as well. In addition, there are other channels like resellers. How are all these customer-facing units coordinated? Or do they have to be coordinated? The next section examines this issue by looking in more detail at Global Services EMEA.

Global Services Organization–EMEA

Global Services EMEA is itself a multidimensional organization. It is about a $12 billion business with sixty-two thousand people plus another fifteen thousand in companies in which IBM has a 50 percent stake or more. The structure is shown on the EMEA chart in Figure 5.3. There are the five business segments that cluster the profit centers: consulting, systems integration, outsourcing, services (availability, customer support), and education. The primary dimensions are the five geographies, which are also profit centers and in which most of the people reside. There is a joint P&L matrix for tracking business segments in the regions. The third dimension is the offerings led by solutions, although some, like hosting services, are in the outsourcing segment. These offerings are also P&L units. In addition there are the usual finance, human resources, and other functions.

The result is a complicated matrix organization. Most of the people have multiple reporting lines. It is possible to be a consultant in the Nordic region working in the banking industry. Furthermore, the consultant could be working on e-commerce offerings in the banking industry. Since the Nordic region is a leader in e-commerce, it is possible for the consultant to get project work in other EMEA regions to transfer leading ideas to those regions. The consultant can be working for the heads of consulting, the Nordic region, the e-commerce offering, and the banking industry.

The salespeople can also have similarly complex reporting lines. The product lines in global services have their own sales forces originating opportunities as well as receiving opportunities originated by the industry customer sets. Why do the product lines have their own sales forces? First is the need for product expertise. A service like outsourcing must be sold by an expert. It is a new product and different from an equipment sale. Outsourcing is a commitment to an income stream over five to ten years. There are risks that need to be managed by the specialists. These specialists work with and become members of customer teams from the industries. There are also small teams from global services dedicated to the six industry sectors, which are available for large opportunities. But the sales forces also call independently of the industry sets. Sometimes a customer wants to add a maintenance contract that was not included in an equipment sale. Also, customers typically want one partner to service their equipment. IBM can receive the service contract from a Hewlett-Packard customer. In fact, through maintenance and outsourcing, IBM global services is the largest customer in Europe for Hewlett-Packard. These sales require customer calls outside the industry sales force.

It is possible that the customer wants to deal separately with the IBM product lines. For example, the education service could be sold to a manufacturing customer as part of an e-commerce offering. That same manufacturer's training and development (T&D) unit may want to contract separately with IBM's education unit for a management development course. The e-commerce offering could be sold to the customer's information technology department and the education to the T&D unit under separate contracts through separate sales forces. In this way, IBM does business with the customer in the way the customer wants to do business with IBM.

The situation becomes more complicated when more channels are added. Education could be sold to a customer through a reseller as part of an offering or as an independent service. Education could be sold to a customer over the Internet or through a call center doing telemarketing. The possibilities are shown in Figure 5.5. The possibility for disagreements and conflicts is multiplied with every channel. Disagreements on customer priority, skilled educator allocation, and price differences immediately come to mind.

The process for dealing with the channel complexity is Omsys and the channels organization. If every opportunity is entered into the system, a complete customer picture can be obtained by all persons dealing with that customer. A common customer code must be used by all parties. IBM has worked hard at creating the discipline to use Omsys. All of its people have been trained, and most business goes through CRM. However, getting joint venture partners, resellers, and partially owned companies to use Omsys still requires some work. This task is the one handled by the channels unit.

Once an opportunity is entered into Omsys, it can be analyzed, prioritized, assigned to an owner, and tracked. The customer account manager in the industries can view all transactions with his customer and can receive credit for all revenues. The account manager can communicate with the other channel participants and coordinate actions. Disputes can go through the normal resolution

Figure 5.5 Possible Channels to the Customer

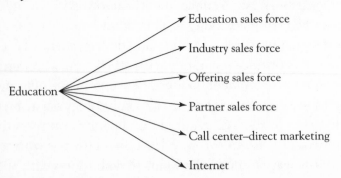

process. But the key is getting the opportunity, indeed all opportunities, entered into Omys. This discussion focused on global services, but similar issues arise in selling software and hardware.

People and Rewards

One of the biggest changes at IBM has been in the area of HR policies. IBM was known for its individual rewards and quota measures: "Beat your quota and go to the Golden Circle." In Europe, the HR policies were mostly country based. Every country had its own payroll system. Country managers felt that they "owned" the talent in the countries. Succession planning based on replacements was used. The reward system was managed by administrators who compared performance to quota. It was a system based on stability and hierarchy.

Just about all of that system has changed. The individual quotas have been changed to group quotas. With the specialization of the sales force, selling is done in teams of industry and product specialists led by an account manager. A team may get a quota for commercial banks in Switzerland. Another team may have a quota for retail banks in the Basel area. The quotas are set around whatever group makes sense for the business.

People are assessed today on the basis of competencies. The assessments are made regarding the potential of people rather than as replacements for positions. The competency model was built with Hay-McBer. The competencies result from studies on what competencies will be needed by IBM managers in the future. The result is an IBM executive leadership model consisting of eleven competencies grouped into four clusters (Exhibit 5.1). Each person is rated on each competency on a four-point scale.

The assessments are done in a variety of ways. The task is managed by executive resources. They identify some twelve thousand people who have potential. The top eighteen hundred are specifically managed on a global basis. The CEO chairs the World Management Council (WMC), which discusses the top 250 people in IBM versus the competency model. A group of young employees

Exhibit 5.1   IBM's Executive Leadership Model

I.   Focus to Win—Competencies that enable leaders to think about IBM's relationship to its customers and the marketplace in order to provide breakthrough strategies for success.

    1. Customer Insight

    Putting oneself in the mind of the customer, seeing the customer's business from their point of view.

    2. Breakthrough Thinking

    Having new insights about how to position their business to win in the marketplace.

    3. Drive to Achieve

    Making continuous improvements in the existing business model (i.e., doing things faster, better, and at lower cost and higher quality) and taking calculated business risks to pursue new market opportunities.

II.   Mobilize to Execute—Competencies that enable leaders to take dramatic, decisive action that energizes teams to rapidly execute against their business strategy.

    4. Team Leadership

    Focusing their organizations on winning strategies through skillful influence and impactful action.

    5. Straight Talk

    Telling the truth, even when it's unwelcome, and acting with integrity, consistent with one's beliefs.

    6. Teamwork

    Working collaboratively with others to run their business effectively.

    7. Decisiveness

    Making tough decisions and acting on them with speed and urgency.

III.   Sustain Momentum—Competencies that enable leaders to sustain results over time by developing priorities, people, processes, and structures aligned with the business strategy.

    8. Building Organizational Capability

    Getting the right people, systems, and procedures aligned with business strategy.

    9. Developing Talent

    Helping others grow and develop to provide long-term bench strength for the organization.

    10. Personal Dedication

    Aligning their personal needs and priorities with the "greater good" of IBM—not the "silo's."

IV.   The Core—The "heart" of the model, what energizes IBM's leaders.

    11. Passion for the Business

    Being excited and passionate about IBM's products and services, its possibilities, and ways it can help customers and the world.

with high potential and some women and minorities are also singled out for individual discussions. Information is obtained from HR-trained people, assessment centers, and 360-degree reviews. The idea is to get a variety of comments and to make assessments in a group discussion context. The industries and the product lines also assess people around the globe in the same team context.

In addition to the global executive resources assessment process, there are other global HR processes as well, including a global job classification system and a single worldwide process for performance management. With the products and industries structure, human resources are becoming more available for pan-European assignments. More people are working outside the countries. The language of the company is becoming English. Roughly forty nationalities are to be found in the Paris headquarters. These centers, like Paris and La Hulpe, Belgium, are melting pots of multinationalism. With many barriers removed, the talent is no longer locked up in country silos. Most of the country managers have been changed to facilitate this transition.

The other feature of HR policies is the increase in variable compensation and the use of stock options or, now, stock grants. The mix of compensation policies varies, but let us look at an industry head in EMEA. This person would have a salary, which in an average year is 50 percent of the take-home pay. The other 50 percent is bonus. That bonus would be based 50 percent on worldwide performance of the industry, 30 percent on EMEA, and 20 percent on the industry in EMEA. This population represents the two sides of the matrix in which industry managers in EMEA find themselves. These proportions represent a large increase in variable pay. But the biggest impact until recently had been stock options. Options were granted to the manager by the HR committee like WMC. Each individual was assigned a percentage from 0 to 200 percent. That means an individual could receive no options or two times the option grant. Today, these options are being migrated to restricted stock grants. The percentage is based on the person's contribution to IBM. Contribution is to account for customer satisfaction and all the unmeasured dimensions of performance like teamwork and helping out a colleague. The option amount varies, but in recent years for many people at the industry level, their annual stock earnings have matched their annual take-home pay (salary plus bonus).

So today, people are assessed on meeting their targets, contribution, and competencies. Many of the HR policies are global and not country based and are more team and less individually based. Compensation is more variable and includes more stock. These assessments are a different set of lenses and are intended to reward, develop, and promote the kind of people who can deliver all of IBM to the customer.

Progress in Delivering IBM to the Customer

IBM has been quite successful in following its strategy of delivering solutions to customers. Its performance on revenues, profits, shareholder value, and customer satisfaction has been good. It now gets less criticism from the "focus enthusiasts," who said IBM should focus like Dell or Cisco. Indeed, Dell, Cisco, and Hewlett-Packard are also going into solutions and copying the IBM business model. It is just as easy to ask, "How well will the focused companies play IBM's game?" IBM believes that 60 percent of its customers want solutions. The price of competing in solutions is managing complexity. How is IBM doing at managing its complexity?

One assessment would be that IBM is having an appropriate amount of difficulty. It is probably attempting to manage more complexity than any other company. It is trying to integrate diverse businesses to serve customers around the world at top speed and at high standards of performance. It has multiple businesses and business models. It has activities in 170 countries, which need to be integrated into solutions for local, regional, and global customers. The integration needs to take place at Internet speed and at performance levels defined by Dell, Cisco, Intel, Nokia, and other more focused competitors. There is no other company facing the coordination task that IBM is. How does it deliver integrated and leveraged speed in the service of customers?

The success achieved so far results from doing a number of things right. IBM chose the right strategy for its customers. It did indeed want solutions based on network-centric computing. And IBM was able to create an organization that could integrate the products and services for these customers. The structure was changed to a front-back model in which the customer-facing industry sectors (front) were able to develop customer relationships and focus. And the product lines (back) developed global scale and excellent products that could be integrated into customer solutions. Reengineered processes for new-product development, supply chain management, and customer relationship management tie the front and back together. A finance group arbitrates the usual disputes about prices and revenue sharing that can paralyze other solutions providers. A customer-focused planning process produces a clear set of priorities. And when the world changes, new priorities can be set by referring issues to dispute-settling bodies like the senior leadership team, which decides quickly. Teams of sales specialists are rapidly assembled to bring knowledgeable people together quickly to serve customers. The quotas are now team quotas. A new higher variable-pay system emphasizes the company, the global business, and then the local business, in that order. Stock awards granted on the basis of contributions and customer satisfaction communicate a common message. New people were brought in to lead the way in new directions. People are selected and promoted based on assessments of competencies. Multiple inputs are gathered in making these assessments. So a number of changes were made to convert IBM into a company that can deliver its whole self to the customer. But the changes are mutually consistent and reinforce each other. All of them produce integrated solutions at high speed for the customer. They are summarized and shown in IBM's star model in Figure 5.6. IBM has touched all elements of the star model. I would argue that this thoroughness is a factor in its success. The issues discussed below arise because not all of the people fit with the new design.

But the changes continue, and the transformation is a work in progress. A company like IBM surfaces issues that are not faced by others when pursuing this level of complexity. The reason is that

Figure 5.6. IBM's Star Model

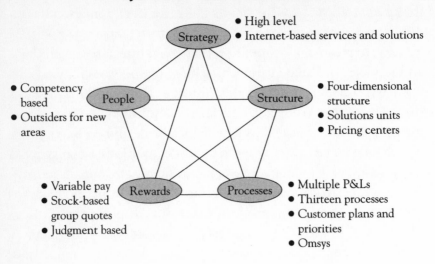

organizations have not been designed before and managers not been developed before to deliver this level of performance for this level of complexity. New design and new development issues arise as a result. The following paragraphs describe the organizational frictions that result.

Some of the frictions are normal matrix issues of any multinational organized around product lines, geographies, and functions. On their management teams are representatives of the three dimensions who view the world through three different lenses. At IBM-EMEA there are people representing customers, solutions, and partners in addition to the normal three views. This multifaceted orientation should give IBM an advantage in seeing a change coming, but only if the multiple views can be resolved on a timely basis. IBM will surface more differences as a result of its multidimensional view of the world. It will also generate more conflicts, putting a premium on rapid management decision making.

At lower levels of the organization, the multiple dimensions mean multiple reporting lines. These multiple reports have always been an issue in multinationals. But the move away from command-and-control cultures—and an understanding of "that's the way it is" in a solutions business—helps people to accept the complexity. But not everyone is there yet. Some cultures accept the multiple reports more easily than others. Through selection and self-selection, people who fit in stay and rise to the top.

IBM's situation pushes the envelope on this issue. Most companies wrestle with two dimensions. IBM's people, like the consultant mentioned earlier, can have three, four, or five reports in a given year. Also a characteristic of matrix structures is that "problems fall." That is, unresolved policy issues, which should be settled at the leadership level but are not, fall to lower levels where the issue cannot be postponed. These become dilemmas for people with multiple reports and multiple unresolved dilemmas. The more dimensions there are in a company like IBM, the more of these unresolved policy issues will arise, and some will drop to subordinates. Usually these people do not have the knowledge and maturity to make policy decisions. So it is natural to see a company struggle with executing multiple dimensions quickly.

Conflicts are easily generated. I have noted that a four-dimensional organization is much more likely to generate conflicts than a two- or three-dimensional one. And the possibilities for conflict increase exponentially. In addition, IBM is in a business that changes every day. There are new technologies, new competitors, new customers, and new ways to go to market. When people face situations they have not faced before, the likelihood of seeing things differently increases.

All of this integration and activity takes place in an environment of high performance standards. Everything has to be done with higher quality, lower costs, and faster. IBM used to be reasonably tolerant of people. Today employees have to perform. There are more casualties as a result. Today one has to be a complete manager. Today one has to show teamwork, be a team builder, be a networker, and communicate. Managers in Europe start the morning communicating with colleagues in Asia and end the day communicating with others in the Americas. Whether employees make their numbers or not, they are assessed on being a total person.

IBM is pushing the limits of what can be done in a large organization with today's talent. It has done a lot of things right. But when systems are pushed to higher levels of performance, the limits to that performance are discovered. IBM is trying to fix these limits.

Lessons Learned

Following are the primary points illustrated by the IBM case:

- The IBM case illustrates the kind of reorganization that is needed to become customer-centric. IBM has identified a strategy that creates value for customers. It has designed a front-back structure that provides a customer-centric front end and a product-centric back end. It has tied the front and back together with business and management processes. And finally, it has completed the design with compensation and human resource practices that align the organization with the strategy.

- One gets a sense of the complexity that needs to be managed if a company chooses to supply solutions of large scale and scope that require integration. However, we need to remember that customers would be left with the task of providing this same coordination if IBM did not do it for them. By taking on the complexity, IBM creates value for customers. By managing this complexity better than its competitors do, IBM creates an advantage for itself that is hard to match.

- The IBM case provides a good example of how formal management processes allow IBM to master complexity. The CRM, Omsys, SalesLink, solutions development, planning, and pricing, to mention just some of the processes, take a lot of the burden off managers.

- Another way to manage complexity is to reduce it through replicable solutions. By productizing a solution, IBM does not have to reorganize for every unique solution opportunity.

- We get some idea of the level of conflict that is generated by putting a customer-centric unit alongside a product-centric unit in the same company. A natural tension results that must be continuously managed by the leadership.

• The IBM experience shows how difficult it is to build a customer-centric organization. After ten years, IBM is still struggling to master the complexity. However, any competitor that wants to match it must repeat the same type of process. Once IBM achieves some mastery, it will have a competitive advantage that has some durability.

6

Alternate High-Level Solutions Companies

In this chapter you will learn:

- About companies in other industries that have evolved to the same front-back structure as IBM.

- That there are variations in the front-back structure. Nokia applies it to a division; Procter & Gamble, like IBM, applies it to the whole company.

- That a successful solutions strategy requires the selection of customers who desire solutions.

- That doing business the way the customer wants to do business causes a complex front end of the structure and value for the customer.

- That Procter & Gamble evolved first in the United States and then moved globally.

- How Citibank evolved into customer-centric organization by building organizational capability first and then changing structure rather than the other way around.

- How to manage the change process itself.

This chapter describes some additional companies that have built high-level customer-centric organizations. The computer companies like IBM are not the only ones that have transformed themselves. Nokia's Network Systems business is an example of a wireless telecommunications equipment supplier that was a product-centric business unit in 1990 and a product- and customer-centric unit in 2000. Procter & Gamble was a product-centric consumer packaged goods company in 1985. By the early 1990s, it had built a customer-centric capability in the United States; by 2000, the global organization was transformed. Citibank and, now, Citigroup provide a service company example—one that took a unique trajectory to arrive at the front-back organization.

Nokia Networks

Nokia Networks' story begins around 1990. At that time, Nokia was a Finnish conglomerate with sales in Finland and the Soviet Union. When the Berlin Wall came down, the Soviet economy collapsed, taking Nokia down with it. When new leadership came in, they focused Nokia on wireless telecommunications and began selling off all the other businesses. They reinvested the funds from those sales in mobile phone products for consumers and network products (switches and base stations) for operators of wireless networks. The phones and handsets were immediately successful. Today, the handset business is about 70 percent of Nokia.

The network equipment business had a tougher time getting started. The network operators in Europe were all state-owned monopolies, which bought their equipment from their national champion suppliers (for example, France Telecom bought network equipment from Alcatel, and Deutsche Telekom bought its equipment from Siemens). The market was tough for newcomers to crack.

These state-owned companies were to provide jobs as well as phone service, so they were staffed with those who designed, installed, managed, and repaired their own networks. They needed suppliers only to provide them with products like switches and transmission equipment. As a result, all of the suppliers, including Nokia, were product-centric companies. The Nokia organization as of the early 1990s is shown in Figure 6.1. The product lines are network systems (switches), radio access systems (base stations for trans-

Figure 6.1   Nokia Networks, Early 1990s

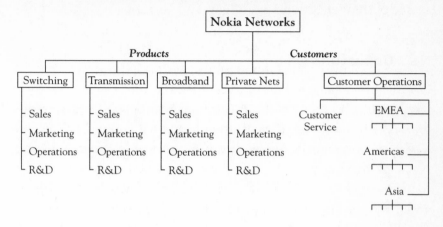

mission), broadband systems (new Internet and other digital systems), and professional mobile radio (dedicated systems for police and emergency networks). Each of those is a fully functional business consisting of sales, marketing, operations, logistics, and R&D.

Customer operations is the customer-facing front end. Until 1999, the customer was local and the structure was geographical. Some are still local, but others are regional and becoming global. The field organization consists of sales and marketing for a geography. The account managers are generalists and sell all products to the network operators, which usually buy all products. The product sales specialists are also in the field and assist the customer account people on sales. A sale can vary from $10 million to over $100 million. These opportunities appear intermittently. Teams form and reform around these opportunities, to bid and to deliver when a bid is won. It is a contract and project business. In Europe there are around 270 customers, but 10 percent account for 50 percent of the business. The other part of customer operations was customer service, which is an installation and repair unit to service the company's equipment under warranty. The sales and service people are all physically located in the countries and work for their product divisions and the field country managers. Nokia Networks was particularly proud of this product-country matrix, which they believed to be a source of their effectiveness.

New Opportunities

Opportunities came as European countries began to deregulate their wireless telephone networks. As each country deregulated, new operators entered the market. In the United Kingdom, Orange and Vodafone entered the market. It was Mobilix in Denmark and Star Network in Singapore. Unlike the state-owned companies dominated by engineers, these start-ups were staffed with entrepreneurs and marketers. Because they had very few engineers and lean operations, they went to the equipment suppliers and said, "How fast can you design and build a network for us?" The product-centric national champions like Siemens and Alcatel responded, "We design and build switches, not networks." Nokia, however, saw an opportunity and replied, "We'll be happy to design and build a network for you." Nokia hired some new people, bought some small consulting firms, and trained and developed some of its own people, and collected them in a professional services organizational unit. Nokia provided technical consulting to the newcomers on the design of networks and purchase of equipment. It also advised on adding and pricing features like call forwarding. It was helping customers to be more effective and profitable, and the more profitable those newcomers were, the more services and equipment they would buy from Nokia. Over time, Nokia added an education service unit to provide training to its own people and also to teach network operations and pricing to customers. It added as well a special unit for project management. Each network design and installation is a big project. Good project managers are scarce, so Nokia began to develop its own. Eventually Nokia began to receive requests from operators to run their networks so that the operator could concentrate on sales and marketing. Today Nokia has an outsourcing unit that runs networks for operators. Its organization in 2000 looked like the chart shown in Figure 6.2.

Figure 6.2 Nokia Networks, 2000

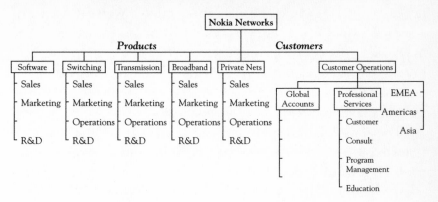

The professional services unit has grown to several thousand people; the various new units are shown in Figure 6.2. Also shown in Figure 6.2 is a global accounts unit. This unit was added in 2000 as the industry was consolidating. The consolidation of the customer has been happening for some time. Originally the cellular phone business was a national or subnational regional business. Cellular companies were granted licenses to operate in a particular geography. One of the licenses usually went to the existing fixed-line telephone company, but it had to create a separate subsidiary so as not to subsidize it. Other licenses went to newcomers. There was an initial period of explosive growth where anyone could make money. But in markets where competition was allowed, prices began falling and the natural shake-out took place. The stronger players bought the licenses of the weaker ones.

Other factors came into play as well. Mobile phones were bought by mobile people. When these people traveled to other areas and used their phones, they were charged higher fees for roaming. The operator whose customer paid these fees received only a small portion of the charge but a large portion of the complaints. Some operators saw the advantage of a single area with no roaming fees. This area was first national, then regional, and now global for operators like Vodafone. They would like to offer a single, seamless global service with a single price.

The Internet connection is another consolidation. The Internet knows no boundaries. People can log on to a Web site from anywhere. Why not make the access easy anytime and anywhere? And to provide this access, operators need to buy new equipment. This investment is large, and only a few have the necessary resources. Consolidation is one way to gain leverage in purchasing power to make these investments more economically.

The consolidation started in stages. Initially cellular was a national business. Then the operators began investing in other countries. They usually took a minority position along with two to five other operators. The operators discovered that they had little control over pricing and purchasing decisions made in these subsidiaries. Some of the stronger players began to buy out others and establish controlling positions. When Vodafone won the bid for Airtouch, the acquisition contest began. Mannesman bid for Orange (in the United Kingdom). Then Vodafone bid for Mannesman. Deutsche Telekom acquired One-to-One (in the United Kingdom). Japan's DoCoMo then took stakes in European companies and in AT&T's wireless subsidiary. Then Cingular bought AT&T Wireless.

As this process continued, Nokia began to form units dedicated to these emerging global operators. Nokia was always organized around the operator customer with its account representatives and country structure. When the customer began to control subsidiaries, Nokia started to use cross-border account managers. The geographical organization saw the operators growing and moving across borders. Then a couple of years ago, Nokia created global account managers. Some were the local account managers who were given global responsibility. Others were full-time global account managers. There were about fifteen global account managers for the largest customers.

When the big acquisitions started, this global account manager structure was seen as insufficient. The global account managers were not recognized by the product divisions and had little authority. Then in September 1999, Nokia created a global relationship management function. It reported to the head of customer operations, who reported to the head of Nokia Networks. With the Vodafone-Airtouch merger, Nokia's management felt a need to get in control of the consolidation. Literally every day, there was an article in the *Financial Times* about a takeover, merger, buyout, or alliance among operators. Nokia management knew the leaders of the operators but needed top-to-bottom knowledge of the customer and its strategic intentions. It wanted to get out ahead and not have to react to the latest customer consolidation. In addition, it wanted to get a jump on third-generation issues. So it was Nokia management, and not the customer, that asked for global relationship management.

The reasons were several. First, Nokia wanted better information and more systematic and continuous contact. There was a lot of contact with some customers. The account manager, country management, product sales, and R&D people all had contacts. But each one would come back with a different answer to the same question at the same customer. In part, the customer was not very coordinated either.

Second, Nokia wanted better information so that it could coordinate Nokia for the third-generation infrastructure opportunity. The operators, after consolidating, would probably standardize their equipment and choose one or two global suppliers. The time that the supplier consolidation would happen would probably be on the purchase of new third-generation infrastructure. The operators would choose suppliers that can coordinate globally and are seen as long-term players. Nokia wanted to be seen by the operators as being in this category. It also needed to know which customers could coordinate their own subsidiaries' buying decisions. Some operators want to make central buying decisions but cannot get their subsidiaries to follow the central decision. Others want a global contract but let their subsidiaries do their own buying.

Both Nokia and the operators want to know the other's technology road map for third generation. They also want to influence these maps to their own favor. Nokia wants the customer to choose its technologies and standards. There will be strategic partnerships in which this information is shared and the partners co-invest in the technologies. There may be some customization of services technologies. Nokia needs to choose which operators will be its long-term partners. Which ones are trustworthy and easy to work with? Which ones will be the winners in the consolidation? On which customers should Nokia place its priorities? There are not many experts on third-generation technology and business aspects. To which customer team should these people be assigned?

The global relationship management unit was created to have Nokia chosen as a preferred supplier and partner. It is to represent both networks and terminals in this effort. The country manager from Japan appointed to lead the unit created a project team to establish the unit's mandate, roles and responsibilities, practices and processes, performance measures, and supporting information systems.

The global account managers will focus on the largest and most important customer accounts. For each selected account, there will be a full-time relationship director and a customer executive, who will be one of Nokia's top executives. The relationship director will report to the head of global account managers and also to the customer executive and the regional vice president from the region in which the customer headquarters is located. The relationship director will lead three teams to serve the customer. First is a core team consisting of the key country account managers, the regional sales representative from terminals and networks, and representatives from technology, marketing, logistics, customer support, finance, the customer executive, and a representative of the customer. Another team is the virtual team that consists of all sales representatives having contact with the customer. The intranet site for the customer will be the primary coordinating device for this group. And finally an extended team will be used when preparing for and delivering customer opportunities.

The core team will prepare the customer plan. The results will be measured by metrics important to the customer. The measures will apply to all core team members, who will receive customer team goals. The virtual team will react to the plan and respond to it. Twice a year, this plan and progress will be reviewed at executive review meetings by top management. In addition to the plan, there will be a customer profile (basic data) and a relationship map showing all contacts from Nokia to the customer.

The role of the relationship director and the teams is to manage the global relationship and build customer satisfaction. They will have new business responsibility and be measured by customer share. And finally they will be responsible for global deals. The purpose is to secure a Nokia-wide mandate and to get acceptance inside Nokia. If the relationship directors are seen as having little influence, they will have difficulty gaining access to the customer, and Nokia is less likely to be seen as a global supplier.

In addition to the usual challenge of introducing a customer dimension on top of the products and geographical dimensions, Nokia has an additional challenge: finding qualified relationship directors. These are people who must be acceptable to the customer, recognized within Nokia, and knowledgeable about the competitive third-generation landscape. Nokia does not have a long history of global account management that would have developed staff internally. On other occasions, companies have hired senior people from the customer's industry. But experienced people from the old monopoly PTTs (post, telephone, and telegraph) do not fit well into the young entrepreneurial Nokia culture. Yet a German is preferred when dealing with Deutsche Telekom, as is a Spaniard for Telefónica and a French native for France Telecom. One approach has been to hire former managers from the national PTT and pair them with a Nokia manager like a former country manager. The PTT manager can teach Nokia the network in the PTT, and the country manager can link to Nokia's internal network.

Nokia started with relationship directors and core teams for the three most important operators. The three will be expanded to about ten. The process proceeded by discussions among the leadership, the building of accounting systems for customer P&Ls, the creation of customer measures, customer intranets and extranets, and customer satisfaction measures.

Salient Points

The Nokia case illustrates a couple of points. First, not all customers want to be provided with solutions. Nokia supplies these customers with products as they desire. But it focuses on the new operators and their desire for solutions and outsourcing. Second, Nokia has developed a customer-centric front-end organization. It has added services units and a global accounts unit to provide solutions, outsourcing, and constant customer interaction with the most important customers. This customer-centric unit has been added to the product-centric units. So Nokia Networks has made the transition to a customer-centric business. The third point is that Nokia Networks has both a product-centric back end and a customer-centric front end. They can coexist, but only with a strong top management to resolve the constant, conflicting issues.

Procter & Gamble

The organizational journey of Procter & Gamble (P&G) provides another example of a company in a different industry making the customer-centric transition. P&G reorganized its activities first in North America and then around the globe. Consumer packaged goods manufacturing companies were originally structured around categories, as shown in Figure 6.3.

In the late 1980s, P&G's retail customers began to change. The volume buying and intelligence acquired through checkout counter bar code scanners at such mass merchandisers as Wal-Mart and Target substantially increased their power. Some of them demanded a single interface, along with just-in-time supply relationships. In contrast, other retailers began to experience considerable variety in the buying habits of ethnic groups within the regions they served. These retailers were moving in the opposite direction from the mass merchants. They were doing less central buying, even moving the buying decisions to the store level.

Figure 6.3   Former Group Structure of Procter & Gamble

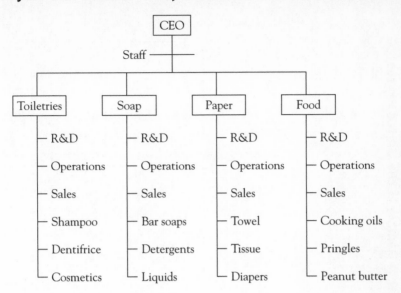

Consumer packaged goods manufacturers have responded differently to these forces. P&G tried to acquire an advantage by adding a front-end structure that enables responsiveness to all types of customers. This structure is shown in Figure 6.4, which illustrates that both a regional structure and a customer structure have been created as the front end of the business.

The regional and customer teams are all multifunctional and staffed by people who come from the product groups. Customer teams are created for customers large enough to justify the effort that want to coordinate operations closely. Some customer teams are located at the customer headquarters. The teams consist of several functions. The marketing people work with customer marketing on analyzing bar code data and using promotions to move product. The salespeople talk directly to the buyers at the customer's merchandising functions. The distribution and information technology people link the logistics functions of the producer and the retailer. And sometimes factory people join the teams to discuss

Figure 6.4 Front-End Structure of Procter & Gamble in the United States

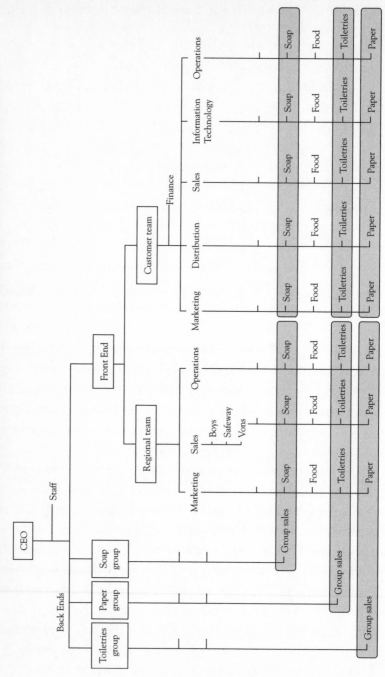

putting on bar codes and prices in the factory rather than in stores. Financial people on both sides discuss ways to speed the turnover of inventory and accounts receivable and minimize cash. The whole cross-functional team works for a customer team leader, who is a senior manager from sales or marketing. The leader of the entire front end is a senior manager with sales and marketing experience.

Product coordination within a customer team is accomplished by the team leader and the top functional managers and by cross-functional teams for each product group. The product team is chaired by the marketing representative. All the product group functional representatives in the front end also communicate with their counterparts in the product groups. These representatives are on two- to three-year rotational assignment from the product groups. Their contacts within the group are kept current throughout the rotations. But in each case, there is a clearly defined interface between products and customers, using the product representatives in the front end.

The regional teams consist of three functions. The marketing function translates the product-marketing message into regional versions. The sales function consists of teams that call on stores where the buying decisions are located. In Southern California, customers that are large enough to justify a team are such retailers as Boys Market and Vons. One store in Monterey Park serves a largely Taiwanese population, and products there must appeal to ethnic Chinese and be in Chinese packaging. The same retailer in Malibu serves the specialized beach community with health foods. The local variety of customers requires responsiveness on a local level. The operations function works with the stores' operations people to set up displays and stock shelves. The functional people on regional teams also can form product teams and communicate with their counterparts in the product groups.

Some customers prefer to do business as they have in the past. For these customers, the company sends salespeople from the group sales forces. The soap salesperson talks to the soap buyers, and salespeople from the paper group talk to the paper buyers. So sales staff can be organized by group (as they have been traditionally), region, or customer. The company has maintained product specialization at the salesperson level, but it has organized them simultaneously by product group, region, and customer. A rotational assignment process develops them to see all three sides of the issue and maintain personal networks.

One strength of this front-back design is that it allows the company to do business the way the customer wants to do business. Different customers prefer different relationships. Another strength of the design is the clear identification of product people and product teams in the front end. These groups can communicate and coordinate within the front end and between the front end and the back end. The structure makes it easy for the customer, but it can be complex for the producer. The same conflicts described earlier exist between customer teams and product lines. In addition, the different interfaces with different customers make things difficult to coordinate. But if the company can manage the conflict and the complexity, it will have achieved a competitive advantage. Competitors cannot easily copy and execute the entire front-back organization.

Over time, most North American customers migrated to the customer team model. The front-back structure was regarded as successful. The leadership then undertook a project to see if the model could be extended globally. When a new structure was found, Organization 2005 was announced in 1998. It consisted of a front end composed of market development organizations and a back end of global business units. The market development organizations were based on geographical regions like North America, Western Europe, and Latin America. The global business units were the product lines, like baby and family care (Paper), fabric and home care (Soap), and beauty care. The number of market development organizations and global business units has varied from four to eight since the announcement as businesses are added or consolidated, and as business grows in a particular region. The structure is shown in Figure 6.5.

Figure 6.5 Organization 2005 at Procter & Gamble

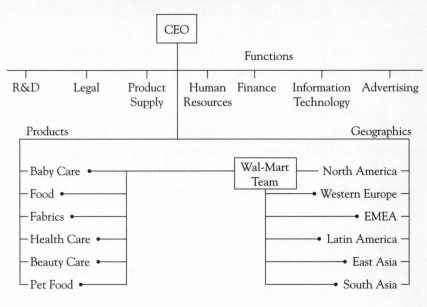

Organization 2005 is a three-dimensional structure. Reporting to the CEO are the usual corporate functions, product lines (global business units), and geographies (market development organizations). The geographical front end shows that most of P&G's customers are local retailers serving local consumers. However, there is a growing international presence on the part of some retailers like Wal-Mart, Tesco, Carrefour, and Ahold, to name a few. P&G has extended its customer team model across borders to service these customers wherever they are. For example, the U.S. Wal-Mart team, some 250 strong, takes the lead in servicing Wal-Mart in all countries in which Wal-Mart has a presence. In the United Kingdom, servicing the Wal-Mart subsidiary (Asda) are about a dozen people. Other teams of a dozen each can be found in Mexico, Brazil, Germany, Thailand, and most other countries where Wal-Mart needs support. In each country, the teams are cross-functional, consisting of sales, advertising, product supply, information technology, and others, and cross–global business units. The team and leaders from the retailer's home country take the lead and coordinate across market development organizations and global business units. The leadership team for Tesco is in the United Kingdom, Carrefour in France, and Ahold in the Netherlands. In this way, the customer teams coordinate service across functions, countries, and product lines.

The P&G example is instructive, as it uses a geographical front-end organization. This structure reflects the existence of local customers, while IBM focuses on global ones. Over time, as the global retailers grow in importance and P&G chooses to focus on them, a front-end structure similar to Nokia's may evolve.

The Capability That Citibank Built

Most companies develop a customer-centric capability and add it to their product and geographical structures. This section describes how Citigroup (then called Citibank) has built its customer-centric unit. It is a good description of the change process used at Citibank's commercial and investment banking unit. In the 1980s, Citibank saw that it was in a position to serve global customers. However, it needed to change its country-based organizations and skeptical country managers and build a capability to coordinate across countries. The change process was a systematic progression through the lateral forms, starting simple and getting increasingly complex. Step zero was at the bottom of the lateral forms, informal coordination. That is, the account managers in countries serving global clients would coordinate among each other. This informal coordination was regarded as insufficient by many global customers.

Step 1: A Few Customer Teams

An initial step to drive the change was to create approximately five customer teams to serve customers around the world. Care was taken to choose the five customers that were most desirous of this global service. The account manager serving the customer's head-quarters was the team leader. In each country where the customer wanted service, one team member was selected. This team then put together an integrated customer strategy and plan to serve the customer and executed it. Two things usually resulted from this effort: the intended purpose of better coordination across countries to deliver integrated service to the global customer and the opportunity to drive organizational change and build organizational capability, which was customer-centric.

The first opportunity is provided by satisfied customers, who can become a genuine force for change. If they were carefully selected, these customers should respond positively to any efforts to better serve them across countries. They will probably respond positively, but they will also indicate that more effort is needed to meet their needs. This outside force—a satisfied customer wanting more—can be used to change country-focused mind-sets. The request for more effort makes them part of the change process.

Another opportunity to expand and build on the capability was already created. With each customer team consisting of 50 to 60 people, between 250 and 300 people have now become aware of and part of the change effort. There are now 300 people trained in cross-border customer strategies; they understand the needs of the global customer and now have cross-border networks and personal contacts. The 300 people themselves will have had different experiences. Most of them should be positive if they were chosen and recruited on the basis of skills and interests. They too can become a positive force for change. Some of these people will enjoy the experience and want more. Some will find that serving local clients is more to their liking and can opt out. For the observant management, the effort is an audition to find cross-border talent. Some people will be good at this new effort and others not. Management that sees its task as identifying new leadership will use the teams as an opportunity to do so. And finally, the effort provides an experience from which to learn and improve. Collecting team members' and customers' experiences and ideas can improve the customer team effort.

In this manner, every change to the formal structure and systems creates two outcomes. The first is to improve the execution of some task. This outcome remains the intended purpose of the change.

The second is the opportunity for management to engage customers in a closer relationship with the company, change doubters' mindsets, train agents of change, build personal networks, select and develop new leaders, and improve the process. Managements that capture the opportunity can use changes to the formal structure and lateral forms to drive and shape organizational change. These two outcomes are produced at each step in the sequence.

Step 2: More Customer Teams

A next step would be to expand from a handful of teams to a dozen or so. Again the firm selects customers that want the integrated service. It can also solicit volunteers or carefully select team members who are interested in cross-border work. The initial team members can solicit their colleagues to join. Usually the firm can make these team assignments attractive. In professional service firms like banks, people are interested in personal growth and opportunity. Working on a team serving a global customer can be a source of learning and development not available with local clients. The multinational customer is usually the most advanced customer. Management can also follow up to see that working on global customer teams is recognized and rewarded in the countries.

Similar outcomes should result from this expanded effort. The difference from the first phase is a larger number of people involved. Instead of a few hundred, this time a thousand or more people are trained in serving global customers and building their networks. A couple of dozen customers are satisfied and asking for more. A critical mass of change agents is being built.

Step 3: Global Accounts Coordinator (Network Integrator)

The next step is to create a position on the management team to coordinate the efforts to serve global customers. At a minimum, this change creates a voice or a champion on the management team for the global customer. Someone of higher status can now appeal to recalcitrant country managers. The coordinator will expand the number of teams again. But perhaps most important, this role can fund and build a customer-focused infrastructure.

One task is to create a common process for building global customer plans and strategies. Initially some experimenting by customer teams is useful. But soon the countries get overwhelmed with fifteen different planning formats. The coordinator can collect best practices from the various teams, initiate a task force staffed with veterans of global teams, and create common guidelines, forms, and processes. It creates a common language for communication about these global customers and their needs. The common process makes it easier for customer teams and country management to work together.

The next step is the design and building of customer-based information and accounting systems. The question always arises, "Are we making any money serving these global customers?" With country-based accounting systems and profit centers, it is usually impossible to tell. Depending on whether the countries have compatible systems, this change can be a major effort requiring central funding and leadership from the global account coordinator. But in the end, the customer teams have information with which to measure their progress, compare their performance with other teams, and demonstrate global profitability.

The two steps can be combined by generating revenue and profit targets for customers in the planning process. The teams can have revenue and profit goals for their global customers. They can have goals for revenue and profit in each country. Perhaps more important, the goals can be added up in each country. Then each country manager can have revenue and profit goals for local clients and for global accounts. The country manager can get credit for—and be held accountable for—targets for global customers in his or her country. The accounting system is important because the costs and revenues from the global customer are rarely connected. For example, an account team in the London office of Citibank worked for a year to win the banking business of a big U.K. firm. The team was successful, but most of the funding for the next few years would be in the North American subsidiary and in a recent acquisition in Australia.

That means that the work plus the costs to win the business were incurred in the United Kingdom, and the revenues were booked in North America and Australia. With customer profit accounting, the United Kingdom can identify the revenues and costs and receive credit. The targets can be adjusted for these disconnects. Thus, in addition to being a champion for the customer, the global accounts coordinator can create the processes and information systems to manage the global customer as well as continue to develop and identify talent and leadership on the teams.

Step 4: A Global Accounts Group

As the number of global accounts and teams exceeds several hundred, the global accounts coordinator role can be expanded into a department or a group. In part for ease of supervision, the customers and teams are grouped into broadly defined industry categories like consumer products, financial services, oil and gas, pharmaceuticals and life sciences, multimedia, and others. But the main reason is customer satisfaction. Customers want bankers who understand their business. Pharmaceutical companies assume their bankers know what the Human Genome Project is all about. So the global accounts activity can be expanded and specialized by customer segment.

The global accounts leadership usually leads an effort to establish a common segmentation scheme across the company. In large countries like Germany, the United Kingdom, and Japan, customer segments were probably already in use. What is important is to have compatible schemes across the countries. Then a one-to-one interface can be established to facilitate communication between countries and within an industry.

The global accounts group is usually expanded by adding global industry coordination. A global industry coordinator is selected for each industry that is common across the countries. Many companies realize the need for global coordinating roles but find few people qualified to fill the roles. But if a company has followed the advice presented in this chapter and used the opportunity created by the initial customer team implementations, it should have developed its own staff by this point.

A Swiss employee in Citibank's Zurich subsidiary can serve as an example. A young banker was identified as a talented performer on work for pharmaceutical companies in Zurich. When a global team was created for Novartis, the banker, who had experience at Novartis, became the Swiss representative on the team. Based on good performance, the banker agreed to an assignment in the United Kingdom, which gave him the opportunity to work in the London financial center. While in London, the banker served as the U.K. representative on the Novartis global team. The next assignment was to lead a large deal for Roche in the United States. The banker was then made vice president and returned to Zurich. From there he was selected to be the global account team leader for Roche. After several years in the team leader role, the banker became the global coordinator for the pharmaceutical customer segment. He was assessed in each assignment for financial performance and knowledge of the pharmaceutical industry as usual. But assessments were also made of teamwork, relationship with customers, ability to influence without authority, cross-cultural skills with customers, and cross-cultural skills and leadership of the cross-border team. Based on these experiences and training courses, the banker was qualified to move into the global coordinator role.

Step 5: Global Accounts Units in Countries

A next step to shift more power to the teams serving global customers is to carve out units within countries and dedicate them to the global customers. The other country units will serve local customers. The global customer units report to the global accounts coordinator and to the local country manager. These country units place dedicated talent in the service of the global customer.

In some small countries, the country management may be reluctant to create a dedicated unit and share in its direction. They may have a surplus of profitable local business and prefer to avoid the multinationals. In these cases, several banks have created joint ventures between the headquarters and the local country management. Usually the dedicated unit is funded from headquarters and staffed initially with expatriates. Then, after a couple of years, the local managers notice that the unit is quite profitable. In addition, they notice that the unit is a positive factor in recruiting. Many new employees are attracted by the opportunity to work with global firms. In this way the creation of a global customer joint venture changes the mind-sets of local management. They eventually take over the staffing and share in the administration of the unit.

Step 6: Customer Profit Centers

A final change is the creation of customers and customer segments as the line organization and profit centers. All of the global units report to the global industry units. The countries manage the local business and serve as geographical coordinators.

This stepwise process was followed by Citibank's commercial banking business. Starting in 1985, Citibank reestablished its World Corporations Group, which managed global corporations across the country profit center structure. It created teams for each global account. The members were called subsidiary account managers, and the leader was a principal account manager. The number of customers qualifying to become global accounts increased to around 450. Citibank created a customer-focused planning system and an accounting system to track customer revenue, cost, and profit across countries.

In 1995, Citibank conducted a strategy study and realized that it was a licensed bank in over a hundred countries. That is, it was in the business of taking deposits and making loans in local currency in over a hundred countries—more than double its nearest competitor (Hong Kong–Shanghai Bank, with around forty-three countries). This presence was a competitive advantage when serving the global customer and one that competitors could not match. Citibank managers chose to emphasize the cross-border bank role.

It would focus on global products, foreign exchange, and cash management for global customers. Each of thirteen hundred global customers became a profit center. These customers were collected into global industry groupings for administration. The customer-focused planning process is now called COMPASS and is placed on an intranet. Thus, in about twelve years, Citibank evolved from country profit centers to customer profit centers and modified its strategy, structure, and processes. It drove the change with formal integrating mechanisms like customer teams and global account coordinators before completing it with the establishment of a new formal structure.

How to Manage the Change Process

In general, management can drive a change process that transforms any existing organization into any new organization using the sequential approach. Each step in the sequence makes an incremental shift in the power structure. The incremental changes are shown in Figure 6.6.

Figure 6.6 Shifting Power Incrementally to a New Structure

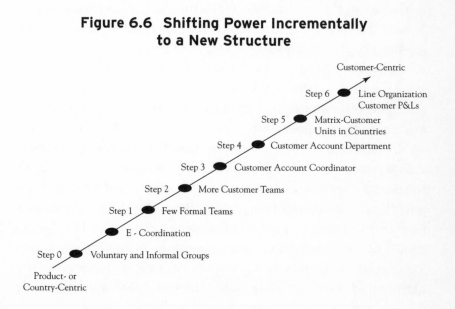

Each increment corresponds to the change in the example. Starting with a few teams and moving to stronger coordinating units, the example described the transfer of power from countries (existing) to customers (new). At each step, new work is accomplished. At Citibank, the new work was cross-country coordination to provide integrated service to global customers. At each step there is also the opportunity to drive and shape the change process. With teams with step 1 and step 2, three hundred and then a thousand people learn about the global customer. They learn how to create strategies that competitors cannot match. A percentage of the participants will become convinced of the direction and lobby the nonbelievers. Through the teams, a thousand people are building networks of personal contacts.

Management's role is to seize the opportunity and drive the change. It may sponsor a formal development program. Everyone working on teams could spend several days in a session with their other team members. In addition to facilitating more learning and networking, managers and customer representatives could attend and get feedback from the participants. But most important is the opportunity for management to select and develop the talent and leadership for the new strategy and structure. By observing and reviewing the teams, management can identify those who have the skills and interest in cross-border work. Who are the best potential team members? Who can be a team leader? Who can develop into a global industry coordinator?

The coordinator roles, introduced and developed in steps 3, 4, and 5, shift more power to the new structure and deliver more service to customers. But the other opportunity is to develop processes and information systems to support the new organization. In addition the coordinator teaches managers about the new strategy. They must shift from managing a portfolio of countries to managing a portfolio of customers. How will they make trade-offs and set priorities? Thus, at each step, management has the opportunity to change the soft factors to support the change. It can develop the talent, build the networks, change the mind-sets, and ultimately create a cross-border, customer-focused culture.

The ultimate step in organizing around the customer is to create a separate structural component for customers. Usually this capability in structural form is added to the company's existing structure, creating a front-back hybrid. Managing this structural form creates its own challenge. Building this customer-centric capability is the other management challenge. The result is an ambidextrous organization generating both excellent products and customer focus.

Conclusion

These three examples expand our repertoire of examples of customer-centric companies that have evolved into front-back structures. Each has followed a different trajectory and arrived at a slightly different structure. Citibank's front end focuses on only global customers and is organized by industry. P&G faces customers who are mostly local and organizes its front end by geography. Nokia is a mixture of some local customers (some remain state-owned monopolies, like Saudi Arabia) and some global ones. P&G seems to be moving toward a Nokia-type of structure. The Citibank example also goes into detail on the change process to get to customer-centricity. It is particularly noteworthy because it illustrates how to build organizational capability. People are trained at each step of the way. Doubters are converted. The information technology and accounting systems are built. Finally, structure is changed after the infrastructure is built.

7

Designing a Customer-Centric Organization

In this chapter you will learn:

- How a company transformed itself from product-centric to customer-centric.

- That strategies should be focused on competitive advantages when choosing solutions and comparative advantages when choosing customers.

- That processes like the planning and goal-setting process, the solutions development process, the pricing and revenue allocation process, the supply chain management process, and the development of a complete accounting system are at least as important as structural changes.

- That management's avoidance of tough decisions will lead to failure to develop a solutions capability.

- That top-down and active management is required to implement a solutions organization.

- That a complete organization design, starting from strategy, and aligned with structure, processes, rewards, and human resource policies, is necessary for an effective and successful solutions organization

This chapter highlights the process of designing an organization to deliver solutions. Although every organization's process is unique, there are some general principles that can be identified. We will follow a company that embarked on the solutions journey and observe the sequence of steps that it took to become a customer-centric organization, which it added to its existing product-centric divisions. This last case shows how one company put it all together.

The Semiconductor Company

The company, which we will call Chipco, was a product-centric company in the semiconductor industry. Over the years Chipco had evolved into a full product line supplier. It started in business by designing and manufacturing discrete semiconductors like transistors and diodes. Then it developed along with the industry and added memory chips and later logic chips. Analogue chips were next. These chips, like converters, would take a continuous analogue measure like temperature or pressure and convert it into the digital code of zeros and ones, which could be processes with digital computers. Chipco then added the chips to do the computing called digital signal processors (DSPs). The last product line was application-specific integrated circuits (ASICs) customized applications.

Chipco adopted the structure that is typical of semiconductor firms. It is shown in Figure 7.1.

Sales and marketing is organized geographically, with field sales and field engineers located in most countries. A few global accounts such as Hewlett-Packard and Siemens were coordinated across the geographies, along with a few large distributors. These sales organizations sold all products and were supported by sales liaisons and product marketing from the product divisions. There was also a manufacturing liaison function in each division. Most of the division talent was in product design. These engineers generated a continuous flow of new products as the process engineers followed Moore's Law: each year they doubled the number of transistors that could be placed on a chip. Manufacturing consisted of the chip fabrication plants, which produced the silicon chips; the assembly and test plants, which put the chips into packages and tested them; and

Figure 7.1 Chipco's Original Product-Centric Organization

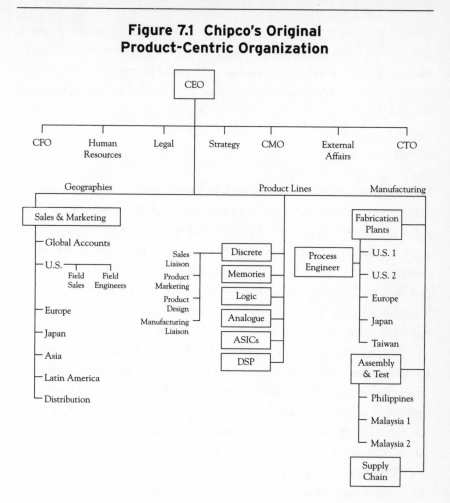

the supply chain function, which managed the flow of materials to and from the plants and eventually to the customers.

Chipco grew with the industry and became a $5 billion company with thirty thousand employees by the late 1990s. As always, Chipco was looking for new sources of growth. With Intel dominating the personal computer industry, most semiconductor producers looked elsewhere to telecommunications, consumer electronics, computer peripherals, and other areas. The digital signal processors division was particularly interested in new markets. The Asia sales manager approached the division general manager about an opportunity in

China: a Chinese company wanted to manufacture wireless hand-sets for the Chinese market, but it had few engineers and no tech-nology. The Chinese wanted Chipco to provide them with a product design (called a reference design), software, and the chips for a wire-less telephone. They would assemble the parts, supply the plastic exterior, and distribute the phones. The digital signal processors di-vision had been exploring wireless applications and had a team of engineers and product marketers working on prototypes. The team accompanied the Asian sales manager to Taiwan to visit an original design and manufacturing (ODM) house. ODMs created original de-signs that were certified by the global telecommunications stan-dards bodies. The Taiwanese ODM could easily create a reference design built around Chipco's digital signal processor. Chipco bought the design, lined up a wireless software company from the United Kingdom, licensed its software, and made the sale of the solution to the leadership of the Chinese manufacturer.

The Chipco design team and the Asian sales manager realized that the customer would need some postsales engineering support. The support would be needed to get the chips, software, and man-ufacturing process to work together at the launch. The digital sig-nal processor division, the U.K. software house, and the ODM could all contribute some engineers at the launch, but the team realized that something more permanent would be needed. Therefore, the sales organization looked for some additional Chinese customers. With the growth in the market, additional customers were located and signed up.

When the first customer launched, the digital signal processor division and the Asian sales organization built a Chinese customer support center. They hired and trained their own field support en-gineers to support their local customer. Chipco thus responded to the realization that a solutions business is support intensive at the local level.

The digital signal processor division then turned its attention to new growth opportunities in wireless handsets. It found that Nokia, Motorola, Siemens, and the big manufacturers were vertically integrated and had their own digital signal processor division or partners. But it became clear that the wireless operators like Vodafone, Orange, and Virgin Mobile were all interested in having their brand on their phones rather than Nokia's. These operators were looking for suppliers who could produce customized private-label phones for them. The project team, now a business operation in the digital signal processor division, along with the Asian and European sales teams, pursued these opportunities. The wireless business operation hired some design engineers from the Western handset manufacturers. These manufacturers had laid off engineers during the downturn, and Chipco was happy to find some competent engineers who understood the whole product. These new engineers could design the customized features into Chipco's reference design for the operators. The Asian sales manager lined up a contract manufacturer from Singapore, which the digital signal processor division approved. Together the wireless business operation, the contract manufacturer, and the U.K. software house supplied handsets to European and Asian wireless operators. Chipco supplied the digital signal processor and combined its other memory, logic, and analogue chips into a chip set to be delivered to the contract manufacturer. Since Chipco was responsible for the handset performance, it had to build up customer support centers in Europe and Asia.

Chipco's handset customers were now all asking for new capabilities. First, they wanted MP3 player modules added to the phones. MP3 software modules could easily be licensed from software houses in the United Kingdom, Denmark, India, and Israel. But Chipco had to add support people in its customer centers to see that everything worked together. Second, the customers wanted a digital camera capability. Cameras were a little more difficult but also presented a larger opportunity. Chipco sold some analogue and logic chips to digital camera makers like Canon and Olympus, so it knew something about the market. But the opportunity was with the computer makers like Hewlett-Packard and Dell. These computer companies did not have the engineering design capability for digital cameras but were interested in providing them to customers and designing links to their PC and laptop offerings. Since they did not want to hire more engineers, the computer manufacturers were interested in buying technology solutions as they moved into consumer electronics. The digital signal processor division and the U.S. sales organization focused on Hewlett-Packard and Dell to provide digital camera technology and chip sets, the core of which was Chipco's digital signal processor.

A digital camera business operation was created within the digital signal processor division from the original business development project team. The new operation brought in some engineers from the analogue and logic product divisions, as well as some engineers with experience in designing digital cameras. These systems engineers could work with the product engineers from digital signal processors, analogue, and logic and provide the integration and knowledge to create a chip set of Chipco's products. In order for all these chip technologies to work together, Chipco also needed to hire software engineers.

Strategy

It is about at this point that the formal strategy decision process is provoked. Up to this time, the digital signal processor division and the Asian and European sales managers had worked informally to launch a solutions initiative. But now the division was hiring more and different kinds of engineers. It was asking sales to create dedicated sales units to address the wireless market and now the digital camera market. Also it was requesting sales to focus on Hewlett-Packard as a global account. Initially the digital signal processor division worked with the analogue and logic divisions to bring in some engineers with the promise of more sales of analogue and logic chips. But it then requested that the analogue division invest some R&D to get its chips to work better and faster with digital signal processor chips in digital cameras. With R&D funds scarce, the analogue division was reticent to invest, so the question became a corporate issue: "Are we in the solutions business?" Are we going to act as one company and integrate product technologies into chip sets for customers that are sold by market segment-specialized sales forces? This decision is the top-down strategy decision that a successful transition to a solutions company requires.

The strategy requires the specific choices of which solutions Chipco will offer and to which customers. The strategy choices of which solutions to offer invoke the usual concepts around competitive advantage. Can Chipco's chip sets provide superior value to those chip sets provided by other semiconductor companies and their partners? The choice of customer or which businesses at a customer to serve raises the issue of comparative advantage. The strongest competitor to a solutions provider is often the in-house capability of the customer. So at Hewlett-Packard, Chipco is not offering chip set solutions to the PC business or to the printer business. In these businesses, Hewlett-Packard has distinctive engineering capabilities. Hewlett-Packard can buy chips and integrate them using its own intellectual property. But when integrating and offering wireless and digital camera technologies, Hewlett-Packard is faced with a choice of building the capability or buying it. With severe cost pressures, Hewlett-Packard and companies like it see an advantage in buying the technology from Chipco, which supplies many customers and has superior scale to Hewlett-Packard. Chipco has a comparative advantage to PC companies in providing wireless and digital camera technologies as a result of its scale. The learning points here are that strategies should be focused on competitive advantages when choosing solutions and comparative advantages when choosing customers.

Returning to the story, Chipco's CEO initiated a strategic review led by the head of strategy. A team and subteams staffed from the divisions conducted a thorough analysis of Chipco's advantages in offering solutions versus other sources of growth. They found that customers generally preferred solutions. There was also a trend to more outsourcing as customers were reducing their own engineering groups. In telecommunications, Lucent, Nortel, and others have laid off engineers and prefer not to hire them back. So the strategy review resulted in a corporate decision to adopt a solutions strategy. It also chose wireless handsets, digital cameras, automotive radio-global positioning systems, Internet wireless connections, high-definition TV, and set-top boxes as the solutions where Chipco had a good chance of developing a competitive advantage. For each solution, it chose which customers would prefer to buy rather than develop their own chip sets.

The choice of strategy led to an examination of how to organize to implement the chosen solutions and address the chosen customers. The human resource department led the organization design effort and visited some computer companies, like IBM, that have had the most experience with offering solutions. The design team, from across the company, laid out the design agenda to choose the structure, the management processes, reward systems, and human resource policies that would facilitate the implementation of a solutions strategy.

Structure

The design of the structure built on the steps that were already taken. The strategic choices pointed the way to extend the existing structure. The first decision was to maintain the existing product division structure. Many customers preferred to buy stand-alone chips, like analogue, ASICs, memories, and so on, as they have in the past. To this structure, the design team needed to add solutions business units for wireless handsets, digital cameras, and, in the future, other successful solutions. The structure is shown in Figure 7.2.

The organization chart shows several additions to the one shown in Figure 7.1. The business operations in the digital signal processor division (originally business development projects) were spun out of the division to become divisions in their own right. To distinguish these profit centers from product lines, they were called business units. They would draw on Chipco's product technologies to be combined into chip sets and increasingly systems-on-a-chip, which are combinations of technologies like digital signal proces-

Figure 7.2 Chipco with a Solutions Business Unit

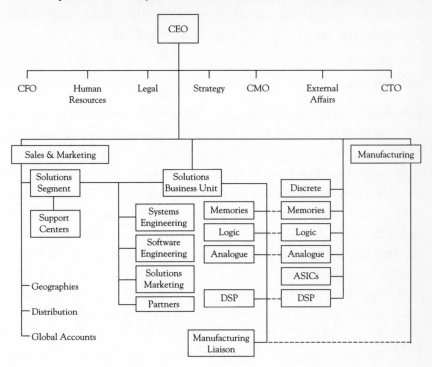

sors and logic that were built into a single chip. Each business unit consisted of engineers from all of Chipco's product technologies, from systems engineering, from the customer solution industry and software engineers. A solutions marketing unit was added to decide on solutions pricing, advertising, positioning, and help with road maps that the customers would want to see. In the sales organization, customer segment units were created for the wireless and digital camera markets. Global account managers were created for the chosen customers in those market segments. These sales units were part of sales and part of the business units. They formed a matrix organization between the geographies and the business units.

The new solutions strategy and organization were announced to the top one hundred managers at the Chipco leadership meeting. The participants were divided into working groups to propose suggestions on how the new units would work with the existing product, sales, and manufacturing units. The leadership responded to questions as well as the working groups' suggestions.

Processes

The next level of involvement of the managers in the company was through working groups for each major management and business process. A process owner was chosen for each process like the planning and goal-setting process, the solutions development process, the pricing and revenue allocation process, the supply chain management process, and others. The processes and the charters for the process teams came from Chipco's experience with combining product technologies into solutions and from benchmarking visits to other solutions companies.

Chipco chose to develop its processes when it introduced its digital camera solution. That is, as it developed its pricing policy for digital cameras, it would create a repeatable process for high-definition TV or set-top boxes. So as the digital cameras solution development process evolved, the process team created an R&D allocation process whereby the business unit could finance R&D projects in the logic product division to adapt its product technology to digital camera solutions. As pricing policies for digital camera chip sets were designed, the pricing process for chip sets was also designed. A pricing center within the finance function was set up to quickly decide on prices for deals and the allocation of revenue back to the product lines like digital signal processors, analogue, and logic.

The delivery of chip sets rather than stand-alone products required changes in the manufacturing function. Manufacturing had to coordinate the production and combination of chip products into chip sets, which could then be delivered as a package to customers. This process required modifying the order entry systems and the supply chain management systems. It also required much more coordination along the supply chain to the customer.

The biggest change was at the leadership level. The leadership team, led by the CEO, was becoming much more active. First, there were many disputes between the product divisions and the digital camera business unit. Often the product division preferred to allocate staff to existing products rather than modify or develop a new product for the digital camera. The CEO and the leadership team supported the "One Company" position to invest in the digital camera. Other divisions disputed the prices for their products in the solution. These disputes served to educate the leadership team in the solutions business. They began to articulate policies for staffing the division-business unit projects and for pricing.

The other management process requiring change was the planning and goal-setting process. Chipco now had market segments, global customers, geographies, business units, and product divisions whose goals needed to be reconciled and aligned. The first task for the process team, which was led by finance, was to build an accounting system so that profit and loss statements could be built for global customers and business units. Then a series of spreadsheets was used to support discussions between the leaders of the various organizational units. A simplified spreadsheet for business units and product divisions is shown in Exhibit 7.1.

Exhibit 7.1 Planning Spreadsheet

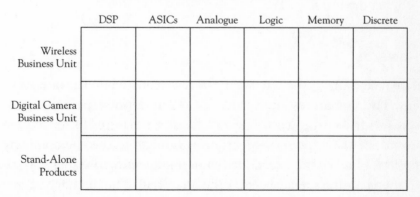

	DSP	ASICs	Analogue	Logic	Memory	Discrete
Wireless Business Unit						
Digital Camera Business Unit						
Stand-Alone Products						

The planning process started with guidelines from the strategy group. Then each business unit and product division put together their proposed plan. Usually the general manager and the business unit or division staff put this plan together. However, the planning teams also used participants from sales and marketing, global accounts and customer segments, product divisions for business units, and business units for the product divisions.

The idea is that the digital camera business discusses and agrees with the product divisions that contribute to the chip set on volumes, prices, revenues, growth, and so on for the planning period. The sales and marketing units also participate in getting agreements. The CEO and the leadership team lead the final completion of the company spreadsheet. The alignment of goals between units is one more top-down element that is added through the planning process.

The implementation of the supporting management processes is when the real strategy change comes alive. When the CEO supports the R&D allocation to digital cameras, supports the assignment of top talent to the digital camera project, supports the pricing policy and forces an alignment of goals between business units and product divisions, the solutions strategy becomes a real strategy. Then Chipco begins to act as "One Company." The tough decisions in the management processes are what create the solutions capability. It is the lack of definitive decisions that leads to failure in other companies.

Rewards

The next design issue is to adapt the reward system to the new strategy. The human resource group looked at options such as Microsoft's shift to using customer satisfaction measures for executive bonuses. At Chipco, the decision was made to use the company profit for half of the executive bonus and meeting the shared goals in the planning spreadsheet for the other half. The human resource group felt that this design would promote the kind of executive behavior that would support the solutions strategy.

People

The staffing choices were made continuously as the strategy evolved. The transition to solutions means the addition of new types of engineers. Chipco added field support engineers to staff the customer support centers and design engineers from the customers' industries to give systems integration knowledge to the business units. And finally, a software engineering capability was added for the customization of designs and the selection of third-party software vendors. All of these new roles were added, and people were recruited, trained, and integrated into the new business units.

Several career planning issues were raised by the transition to solutions business units. The business unit leaders were initially filled with the engineering-oriented project leaders from the digital signal processor product line. This selection helped forge a key link with the digital signal processor unit. These project leaders led the new business development effort into the new solutions markets. But in the future, when more in-depth knowledge of the customer application will be needed, marketing people in the customer segments or managers from the customers' industries might be a more effective source. At lower levels, links are needed between the business unit and product lines contributing technologies to the chip sets. Another link will be between the business unit and the customer segment in sales. Rotational assignments are an effective means of forging links and preparing the next generation of leaders for the business units.

The other major assignment for human resources is training for solutions. The leaders and people at key interfaces need to be trained in the new strategy and new processes for solutions. These training sessions will be good occasions for building relations between sales, business units, and product divisions, as well as educating the key players. So training will be a key activity in the change process to solutions.

Conclusion

Chipco completed the redesign of its organization with the human resource department implementing the training program. It started with strategy and then completed the star model design by moving from strategy to structure to processes to rewards to people. A summary of the complete design is shown in Figure 7.3.

The strategy is now the product strategy plus selected solutions for selected customers. The structure is still the product divisions and geographical sales force plus business units and customer segments in sales. The biggest change is to the management processes. Accounting systems for profit and loss for the business units have been added. Top management is more active in reconciling plans for customer segments, geographies, business units, and product divisions. Business processes have been added for solutions development, pricing, ordering, and supply chain management. The reward system has been modified to reflect a One Company bonus, and at the same time to reinforce the links between business units, product di-

Figure 7.3 Chipco's Solutions Star Model

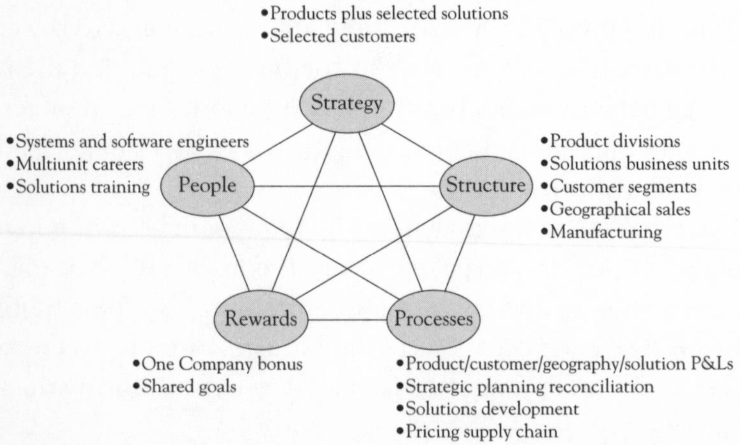

- Products plus selected solutions
- Selected customers

Strategy

- Systems and software engineers
- Multiunit careers
- Solutions training

People

Structure
- Product divisions
- Solutions business units
- Customer segments
- Geographical sales
- Manufacturing

Rewards
- One Company bonus
- Shared goals

Processes
- Product/customer/geography/solution P&Ls
- Strategic planning reconciliation
- Solutions development
- Pricing supply chain

visions, and customer segments. And finally, new people have been added to new engineering groups. The career paths for these people have been redesigned to generate leaders for the new business units. The design is a complete design for this phase. It was led by the top and provided the initial top-down element of leadership that will characterize the company.

Learnings and Salient Points

Following are the primary features that are illustrated in the Chipco case:

• Chipco followed an evolutionary strategy to enter the solutions business. Its first attempt was a light version of a solution built around the digital signal processor chip and local support, but with partners providing the design and the software. Next, it brought in more of its own chips and chip sets and its own software and designs. It eventually moved to complete solutions on the strategy locator. With the addition of a digital camera, MP3, Internet connections, and so forth, a complete wireless hand set was provided to customers who wanted these complete solutions.

• As the solution evolved, so did the organizational unit implementing it. At first, the informal relations between the Asian sales manager, the business development unit in the digital signal processor division, and the division general manager put the deal together. When the solution grew to medium and then to complete, the project team became a business operation within the digital signal processor division and then a separate business unit reporting to the CEO. The more complex the solution and the higher the volume, the stronger the profit center needs to be in order to manage the solution.

• As with many other strategic changes, the initial steps do not come from the top management. In the solutions business, the salespeople encounter customers who want to buy solutions, not just stand-alone products. When some of these salespeople meet managers from the product units who are looking for new business opportunities, a light version of solution can easily result. It is good change management practice for leaders to find and nurture these experiments, help them hire software engineers, and talk with partners and customers. These experiments create some momentum, which can be captured in the change process when the decision is made to start with full-scale implementation.

• Informal change initiatives inevitably encounter barriers, which require top management power and authority. Usually solutions units encounter the product units. Initially, product units are interested in the incremental business that results from solutions sales. But when the solutions units request modifications to the products that are not in the product units' plans, progress can stop. Human resources may not have job titles for software engineers or field support engineers. They may not have a salary structure for them. And human resources itself may not have the people available to redesign the jobs and salary structures for the solution units. At this point, the company needs to decide whether it is going to be a solutions provider. If the decision is yes, then an organization redesign will be required.

• As at Chipco, this is the time to engage the entire leadership and key managers. The strategic decisions revolve around which solutions to offer to which customer. The leadership will have to ask questions such as, "Which solutions draw on the company's skills and competencies? And which ones will provide a competitive advantage? Which solutions do customers want? And which ones provide a comparative advantage over the customers' own in-house capabilities?" These questions were addressed by Chipco and resulted in specific choices of both solutions and customers.

• The structure decision was relatively straightforward as it built on the project and operation structures of the earlier initiatives. The separate business unit design allowed the wireless and digital units to create their own unique business models. Each solution has its own time cycles for product development and life cycle. Separate units for each make sense. The sales unit is a matrix structure. The customer segments for each solution have salespeople who can call at the executive level to get the sale of the larger solution. The segments can also ask the global sales infrastructure to call on local and global accounts around the world.

- A best practice demonstrated by Chipco was the major effort to create the management and business processes to support a solutions business. Solutions businesses are process intensive. Solutions companies have the planning process, the new-product-development process, and supply chain management process that product companies have. In addition, solutions companies require a reconciliation of business unit and product division plans, a solutions development process, a solutions pricing process, and an enhanced supply chain process. Chipco appointed a process owner and a process design team for each process. But the really effective practice was the combination of the process design effort with the implementation of the digital camera solution and the continuous involvement of the leadership. As the solution was designed for the camera, the process was designed. And as disputes arose, management saw that they were resolved on a timely basis.

The reason that this combination was such a good practice is that management leads a solutions company through the processes. A continuous stream of contentious issues arises over prices, R&D budgets, partners, and other issues. By beginning the implementation through process involvement, management learns about solutions, learns how to handle the conflict, manages the change, and models the future behavior. Their behavior shows the centrality of management by process.

- The last lesson is that Chipco created a complete design. It started with strategy and matched it with an organization aligned around structure, processes, rewards, and human resource practices. Chipco created a complete design and managed the change process until the design was in place.

8

Leading Through
Management Processes

There have been repeated references throughout this book for the need for strong corporate leadership. Indeed, the discussion of the failure experiences directly attributed those outcomes to the lack of strong leadership. So if it is critical in customer-centric firms, how does leadership get exercised? In a quick answer, it is through the company's management processes. The front-back organization requires the addition and successful execution of three additional management processes. This chapter describes these processes based on the observation of the best practices taken from the case study companies. These processes are unique to front-back structures. But before describing the leadership role in these processes, let us review the leadership in managing any strategic change.

Leading Strategic Change

Introducing a customer-centric organizational unit into a product-centric company is like introducing diversification, global expansion, or any other strategic change. Some key players will support it, while others will not, and still others may resist. It is the task of leaders to create a sense of urgency and to enroll the key players in the discussion and debates in order to have them shape and buy into the new direction. There are plenty of books and frameworks for leading change (see Beer and Nohria, 2000, for example). The point is that leaders need to confront the resisting key players and resolve the conflicts that accompany any strategic change. Leading the confronting and resolution of these conflicts requires strong leadership.

A second aspect of leading any strategic change is to see that the change is comprehensive. That is, the leaders must see that all of the policies of the star model have been changed to align with the strategy. Simply adding a customer-centric unit to the structure will not work. All of the processes are still product-centric and not compatible with the new unit, or are even antagonistic to it. Indeed, it is when the funding decisions for solutions are given to the customer-centric unit that the change in power becomes clear and concrete. Then the real resistance appears. This change in funding is the opportunity for confrontation and the exercise of leadership. By completing the design of the organization, all of the pockets of resistance can be flushed out and resolved. Everyone in the organization will see the clarity in the newly aligned organization.

The third aspect of managing strategic change is the management of conflict. Conflict is inherent in any major change and needs to be managed as such. But conflict is also a natural part of the day-to-day management of a front-back structure, which delivers solutions. The customer-centric front end is on the side of the buyer, while the product-centric back end is on the side of the seller. A business unit will want to pursue its unique product opportunities rather than play a subordinate role in a solution. Pricing, priorities, and talent allocation all generate an unending stream of conflict-laden issues. There are two things that effective leaders do. First, they legitimize the conflict. Too often conflict is seen as a problem. In a front-back organization, the appearance of conflict is a sign that the strategy is working. Leaders make differences of opinion and conflicts a natural part of the business day. Second, they lead a process that results in a thorough airing of the issues and a timely resolution of them. Like change, managing conflict is a well-researched issue (Eisenhardt, Kahwajy, and Bourgeois, 1997).

The other key feature of the organization design for a front-back organization is the management and business processes that link the front and back. It is in these processes that the leadership exercises its strong role and leads the resolution of the inevitable conflicts.

Linking Processes

Management processes are a critical factor in the successful implementation of front-back structures. The reason is that there are so many issues on which the front and the back will have different positions. The processes are designed to channel these issues to the right forums, support them with the necessary information, and see that the right players are around the table or the speaker phones. As a result, the front-back organization of a solutions provider will have three types of additional processes. The product-centric company has a strategic planning process in which business unit plans are reviewed and prioritized. The solutions provider also has business unit plans. But it also has customer or customer segment and solution plans. These two types of plans need to be reconciled with the business units into a single company plan. The product-centric company has a product development process. The company implementing a solutions strategy has a product development process as well as a solutions development process and a product portfolio process. A stand-alone product provider has an order fulfillment process. The solutions provider has an order fulfillment process as well as an opportunity management system for responding to large solution applications. So the solutions strategy company is more process intense. Let us look at these three types of management processes and see how leaders are to perform their strong role.

Reconciling Strategies

In addition to product strategies, the solutions company must generate customer and solution strategies. At IBM, the plans and strategies are created for servers, desktops, storage units, database software, Lotus software, and other products. There are also strategies for a thousand global customers, which are aggregated into industry groups. Within each industry, the customers are prioritized according to profitability. Then the customer and solution strategies must be reconciled with the product strategies. A product general manager may feel that a customer unit is not featuring the manager's product line as it should. Another product general manager may want to opt out of what appears to be an unattractive solution. There are many opportunities for priority disputes between product and customer managers as well as across product managers. Usually top management performs the reconciliation using a spreadsheet like the one shown in Figure 8.1.

Management first encourages product, customer, and solution managers to work out their priorities. There is a product manager for each row and a customer or solution manager for each column. If differences cannot be resolved, management intervenes with the involved managers or with a larger group representing the leadership, the product managers, and the customer and solution managers.

Either way, the leadership emerges with a spreadsheet with the joint goals for the product lines and customer segments. The purpose of the spreadsheet exercise is to align the goals of the front and back of the organization. They both are to have the same goals.

Figure 8.1   Spreadsheet to Reconcile Solution and Product Plans

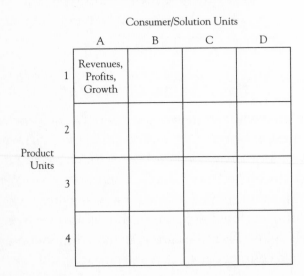

Of course, the plan starts to change no sooner than it is completed. In this case, the leadership convenes a session with managers of the rows and columns of the spreadsheet, and they hammer out a new plan. The frequency of these revisions fits with the time cycles of the market. The leaders of a stand-alone product business can meet and resolve issues with one business unit at a time. The leaders of a solutions provider must convene the right players and resolve issues around the table. The strength to manage this team process is a different leadership requirement for the solutions provider. And the spreadsheet planning process is the forum for the exercise of the required leadership.

The difficulty of managing this process varies directly with the complexity of the solution. *Medium level* means that fewer managers must gather around the table than at high-complexity companies. The medium-complexity company combines fewer components, and they are not as tightly coordinated. The high-complexity company has more managers and more different managers seated around the table. And the more tightly integrated the products are, the more tightly coordinated must be the managers of those products. Different solutions strategies will create different requirements for the planning process and for leadership.

Portfolio Planning and Solutions Development

Every company has a product planning process. Solutions providers have a portfolio planning and a solutions development process as well. Each product unit develops its own products, but each unit's products must work together with the products of other units to provide a solution. The strategy dimension of component integration is important in determining how much effort must go into planning the entire portfolio so that the products will work together. For example, if Nokia is going to offer third-generation equipment, it must have switches and transmission products, software, consulting practices, and customer service contracts as well as handsets that all work together using third-generation technology. The product units cannot independently develop their own product lines without a dialogue. Again, a strong top management team is required to guide the portfolio planning process. The Nokia software product business may want the freedom to challenge Microsoft. However, Nokia will also need a totally integrated product line in order to provide customer solutions. Through the portfolio planning process, the software and other product groups have to develop a strategy that advances their product line and integrates the products into solution offerings.

In addition to developing products, a solutions strategy requires a solutions development process. There are two aspects to this development process. The first is the choice of what solutions to offer. Usually the solutions providers, like IBM and Sun, choose solutions that can be replicated. Replication then requires a process to create a solution that can be sold to other customers. If every solution is unique, the company cannot make much money on them. It needs to invest up front and then replicate the solution to get a return on its fixed investment. Sun uses its planning process to reach agreement on which solutions it will provide. The solutions unit creates teams of five or six people for each chosen solution such as portals, CRM, and e-markets, among many others. The unit also chooses which solutions it will not provide.

The second aspect is an explicit process, like the new-product-development process, to develop a replicable solution. Usually a solutions provider works with a lead customer and invests in the solution so that it can be sold to other similar customers. IBM, for example, tries to start with Swedish banks for its financial services solutions in Europe. It believes that innovation starts in the north of Europe and moves south. Sun uses its i-Force process, a step-by-step process starting with determining a customer strategy to provide certain customers with a jump-start to get on the Internet. Sun uses its Ready Centers to gather people from the customer, its partners like EDS, and its own field marketing solutions unit. The process typically starts with a lead customer suggested by an account manager or partner. Upon approval of the project from the solutions group, a team gathers in a Ready Center to create an integrated stack, as shown in Figure 8.2, for the customer's application. The partners are also selected for applications and are certified in the i-Force process. Upon implementation, the solutions team documents the solution and trains and creates solutions champions in the field marketing regional units. These champions assist account teams in selling the solution to other customers and leading through the i-Force process for solution.

Opportunity Management Process

The third key management process is the opportunity management process. Solutions opportunities appear from customers and require a proposal. Then if the opportunity is captured, the proposal must be implemented. The more complex the solution is, the larger the proposal and execution teams must be. The more resources that must be

Figure 8.2 Sun's Integrated Stack

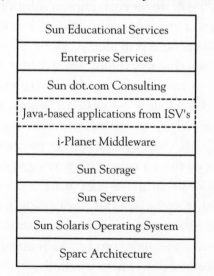

| Sun Educational Services |
| Enterprise Services |
| Sun dot.com Consulting |
| Java-based applications from ISV's |
| i-Planet Middleware |
| Sun Storage |
| Sun Servers |
| Sun Solaris Operating System |
| Sparc Architecture |

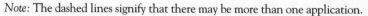

Note: The dashed lines signify that there may be more than one application.

marshaled and the greater the need for a strong project manager, the more complex the pricing decision and revenue allocation to the component products must be. Again, the more complex solutions strategies create the greatest challenges to the leadership.

The best example of an opportunity management process was described in Chapter Five for IBM as Omsys. In matching resources to opportunities, Omsys initially relies on two products from the planning process. One is the customer plan in which the big opportunities are usually identified and resources earmarked for them. However, the exact timing of a proposal acceptance is usually unpredictable, and the size of the project is usually larger or smaller than anticipated. At this time, the opportunity owner uses the second product or the priority assigned to the customer to gather the additional or new resources. Owners for top-priority customer opportunities have better access to resources than those for low-priority customers do. If disputes or shortages arise, these issues become agenda items for the regional leadership teams. These teams give the overall guidance and make decisions about the assembly and disassembly of teams for opportunities. The European leadership team at IBM meets weekly but can gather more frequently when there is a need for real-time staffing of projects.

The challenge of implementing regional and global talent allocation processes is in accessing all the information needed to get a good match between the opportunities and the talent. The decision-making group needs to know the set of opportunities available, the scope of work at the projects for these customers, and the nature of the talent available. It is the information about the talent that is particularly challenging. Most management teams are experienced at allocating money from a total company perspective. But talent involves three issues that make allocating it on a company-wide basis difficult. For starters, a dollar equals a dollar. But a software programmer does not equal a software programmer. A good programmer can be ten times more productive than a mediocre one. So the decision makers need to know the individuals who are invaluable. But there may be hundreds or more people in the talent pool.

Second, dollars do not care if they are spent on R&D or advertising. But people care very much where the project is located and whether it is challenging. The top-down assignment of critically skilled people to projects that they do not like will cause them to leave and join a competitor. So the decision makers need to know the work preferences of the critical people. And finally, dollars do not care with which dollars they are combined to fund an initiative. For people, their coworkers are important. Again, the decision makers need to know something about the chemistry among key team members. These factors are all important to the effective functioning of opportunity teams.

Some firms try to capture as much of this information as possible. Some of it can be captured in formal information databases to create company "yellow pages" for talent that can be accessed by decision makers. But much of it cannot be captured. So in order to bring all the data to the table, some consulting firms increase the number of people at the decision-making meeting. Ernst and Young (E&Y) Consulting would convene a regional task force for one or two days if needed to match talent to opportunities. Like other consulting firms, E&Y used scheduling managers at all of its large offices. For most projects, the account managers and scheduling managers can arrive at acceptable staffing plans for projects. But in the late 1990s, there was a shortage of programmers who knew the SAP application language. Then E&Y, at the initiation of the scheduling managers, would convene a task force when shortages developed. It would gather people who knew the customers, the projects, and the talent specialties. It would even include some of the key specialists in the meeting. These people could choose assignments or have a voice in the assignments that they felt were attractive. The task force could involve thirty to forty-five people in matching resources to opportunities. In this manner, the firm was able to get a total perspective on the set of opportunities, the business priorities, the nature of the projects, and the needs and desires of the talented people. (E&Y even experimented with a spot market for an SAP programmer for a week.)

These real time talent allocation processes are the current challenge for solutions firms. It is difficult to get a total company perspective and also know the details of preferences of talented people and the chemistry of combinations of them. Yet this information is exactly what is needed to satisfy important customers and motivate and retain those who service those customers. The consulting firms and investment banks are probably the most advanced in this area. The solutions providers need to advance their management teams to this level. Most management teams are used to deciding global issues on a periodic basis, not the required real-time basis. They have learned to discuss talented people in assessing promotion needs of the company and development needs of the top 150. But matching talent to the top opportunities in real time is a new challenge for them.

Conclusion

The effective solutions providers are those with strong leadership teams that confront and resolve the continuous flow of contentious issues. These conflicts are channeled into three key management processes for discussion, debate, and resolution. These processes are the strategic reconciliation of product and customer plans, the product portfolio, and opportunity management processes. These processes are the forums for the exercise of strong leadership.

References

Beer, M., and Nohria, N. (eds.). *Breaking the Code of Change*. Boston: Harvard
    Business School Press, 2000.

"Breaking the Keiretsu." *Computer Business*, Sept. 2001, p. 25.

Christensen, C. *The Innovator's Dilemma*. Boston: Harvard Business School Press,
    1997.

Day, G. *Market Driven Strategy*. New York: Free Press, 1990.

Day, G. *The Market Driven Organization*. New York: Free Press, 1999.

Eisenhardt, K. M. Kahwajy, J. L., and Bourgeois, L. J. "How Management Teams
    Can Have a Good Fight." *Harvard Business Review*, July-Aug. 1997,
    pp. 77–85.

Galbraith, J. *Designing Organizations*. San Francisco: Jossey-Bass, 2002.

IBM. *1998 Annual Report*. Armonk, N.Y.: IBM, 1998.

Kehoe, L. "Long Live e-Business." *Financial Times*, Mar. 6, 2002, p. 9.

Narver, J. C., and Slater, S. F. "The Effect of a Market Orientation on Business
    Profitability." *Journal of Marketing*, Oct. 1998, pp. 20–35.

Peppers, D., and Rogers, M. *The One to One Future*. New York: Currency/
    Doubleday, 1993.

Peppers, D., and Rogers, M. *Enterprise One to One*. New York: Currency/
    Doubleday, 1997.

Peppers, D., and Rogers, M. *One to One B2B*. New York: Currency/Doubleday,
    2001.

Reicheld, F. F. *The Loyalty Effect*. Boston: Harvard Business School Press, 1996.

Selden, L., and Colvin, G. *Angel Customers and Demon Customers*. New York:
    Portfolio, 2003.

Seybold, P. *Customers.Com*. New York: Times Books, 1998.

Seybold, P. *The Customer Revolution*. New York: Crown, 2001.

Treacy, M., and Wiersema, F. *The Discipline of Market Leaders*. Reading, Mass.:
    Addison-Wesley, 1995.

Vandermerve, S. *Customer Capitalism*. London: Nicholas Brealey, 1999.

Wiersema, F. *Customer Intimacy: Pick Your Partners, Shape Your Culture, Win To-
    gether*. Encino, Calif.: Spurge Ink! 1998.

Index

MEDICAL LIBRARY
NORTH MEMORIAL HEALTH CARE
3300 OAKDALE AVENUE NORTH
ROBBINSDALE, MN 55422-2900

Galbraith, Jay R.   HF5415
Designing the customer-   G148d
centric organization

15888

MEDICAL LIBRARY
NORTH MEMORIAL HEALTH CARE
3300 OAKDALE AVE. NORTH
ROBBINSDALE, MINNESOTA 55422